Reading through Galatians

Reading through Galatians

C. R. Hume

SCM PRESS LTD

0 334 02705 5

First published 1997 by
SCM Press Ltd
9–17 St Albans Place London N I ONX

Typeset at The Spartan Press Ltd,
Lymington, Hants
Printed in Great Britain by
Biddles Ltd, Guildford and King's Lynn

Contents

Foreword

This book has been written with the aim of encouraging ordinary Christians to study the Bible in a straightfoward and sustained way. I shall try to explain the meaning of every verse wherever necessary (if that is possible). Sensible theological discussion can follow only once the meaning of the original document has been established. The layman or amateur looks to the commentator primarily to explain the text, and can be discouraged by a guide that is overly devoted to discussing theological issues. Unfortunately, sometimes the meaning of the text is not immediately apparent, and sometimes there is no agreed interpretation. The temptation in such cases is to fall back on to a personal theological position in order to establish a particular interpretation.

To understand the text it is necessary to consider what the letter meant to a first-century Christian. In other words, we must concentrate on its original meaning, putting ourselves into the mind of the original recipients, rather than trying to force it into a contemporary context. Of course, we will be led on to consider what the work means to us and how we should respond to it, but we cannot do that unless we are prepared to establish the original meaning first. It is also important to study a whole work and not just short selections from the New Testament. Sustained study is essential if we want to mature in our understanding of the Scriptures. Such an approach requires some discipline and a willingness to explore the meanings of key words and concepts not only in the NT but also in the

Greek-speaking world of the first century. Hence certain Greek words are examined in detail in this guide, but they appear in a form that can easily be read by those who know no Greek.

This guide can be used by individuals studying on their own, but it is more rewarding to study the letter in a group. The leader of the group may consult the commentary when preparing a passage for discussion, or, where resources permit, it can be used by individual members of the group. It is a positive advantage to bring different translations to the group meetings. The differences between these versions often start the discussion going. To make the study even more meaningful and enjoyable one should try to involve people from other churches. In an ecumenical setting it is remarkable how unifying the study of scripture can be. This may be the biggest surprise of all.

This book arose from a course held in Monmouth over four evenings, but it is quite a rush to get through the whole of Galatians in such a short time and grossly unfair to St Paul.

Introduction

Authorship and date

It is generally accepted that Paul wrote this letter. The personality of the author blazes out of every sentence. It was written by a man whose deep feelings about his subject are clear to the most casual reader. The heightened emotions which frequently make his thoughts so difficult to follow are characteristic of Paul's approach. Furthermore, the parallels with other writings of Paul, particularly the letters to the churches in Rome and Corinth, are most striking, as we shall see when we study the text. In the prologue of his commentary on Galatians Jerome observes the similarity of the subject-matter in the letters to the Romans and the Galatians but points out the difference in the tone of the latter, 'rebuking rather than teaching', and notes that the letter is 'the kind stupid people could understand', with everyday expressions and language. That should give us some encouragement when we are trying to follow the arguments Paul uses in the course of the work.

Dating of the letter, however, is a more contentious matter. The scholars who are inclined to date the letter early tend to be those who see problems in reconciling the account in Acts 15 of Paul's visit to the church in Jerusalem with Paul's own account in this letter. Incidentally, this link with Acts makes the letter unique. No other work of Paul gives us such an opportunity to compare his account with another contemporary document in some detail. Most commentators are inclined to set the date of this letter around 57/58, and assume along with such early scholars as Victorinus (around 360) that it was written from Ephesus. It is possible that it was written from Corinth. Some commentators such as Jerome (late fourth century) think that it was written from Rome and some early manuscripts of the letter add a note to this effect. But the close links between our letter and those to Rome and Corinth must be due to the fact that they were written about the same time and therefore it is unlikely that either Rome or Corinth could be the place from which Paul wrote this letter. It is even possible to argue along with Lightfoot that Galatians can be placed chronologically between II Corinthians and Romans due to the way that it seems to reflect an intermediate position in the development of the arguments found in all three letters. The problem of dating will be picked up again in the notes.

Who were the Galatians?

The inhabitants of the central Anatolian state of Galatia were descendants of the Celts who had invaded Greece around 279 BC. Their more remote ancestral cousins around 390 had even conquered Rome. The term **Galatai** was used originally to denote those Celts who lived east of the Alps. Indeed, Gallia and Galatia are philologically speaking closely related names.

Having conquered most of Asia Minor, the Galatians settled down and gradually became less warlike. They were defeated by Attalus I of Pergamum in 230 BC, and by Rome in 189. In 25 BC Galatia became a Roman province. Although conquered they preserved their tribal structure and, while mixing with Greek and Phrygian natives, still spoke a Celtic language. Jerome[1] makes the interesting observation that in addition to Greek they spoke a form of Celtic closely related to that spoken by the Treveri in northern Gaul, *propriam linguam eandem*

---

[1]*Commentary*, 430.

paene habere quam Treveros. Certainly the names of places and individuals in Galatia frequently display their Celtic connection. For instance the great council of the Galatian people met at a place called Drynaimeton, 'the Oak Temple'. 'Nemeton' is well known in Britain and Gaul as the name for 'temple', and the association of oak groves with Celtic religious practices was also noted in the western Celtic countries.

Josephus mentions[2] that 2000 Jewish families had been settled in the area by Antiochus III early in the third century BC. Could this be one of the factors responsible for the strong Jewish influence on the Galatians of our letter? Jewish synagogues could be found all over this region, and it is clear from the account of Paul's travels in Acts that there were many Jews living in the area. It is an intriguing fact mentioned by Pausanias writing around AD 150[3] that the inhabitants of the Galatian town of Pessinus did not eat pork. This is probably not evidence of Jewish influence but might at least account for the fact that some Jewish dietary laws were already acceptable to them.

We are on uncertain ground when we try to define Galatia geographically. Galatia as a Roman province includes Galatia proper with its tribal capitals of Tavium, Pessinus and Ancyra, and also Pisidia and Lycaonia, with their towns of Antioch (Pisidian Antioch, of course, not the more famous Syrian Antioch referred to below), Lystra, Derbe and Iconium. Pisidia and Lycaonia were visited by Paul at least three times, but we are not specifically told that Paul visited Ancyra, Pessinus or Tavium. The most we know comes from the statement in Acts 18.23, 'he went through the Galatian land and Phrygia in order, strengthening all the disciples'.

Are the recipients of Paul's letter to be sited in all these towns or was he only addressing those in Pisidia and Lycaonia? Could

---

[2] *Antiquities*, XII, 148–153.
[3] *Description of Greece*, VII, 17. 5.

the audience be located in the north-eastern corner of Galatia, as has been suggested by Murphy-O'Connor?[4] In the absence of evidence it is a question we cannot answer with confidence.

The central theme

This letter was written in response to a problem developing in the churches of Galatia, but a problem which was probably occurring in many areas, namely the tendency for Christians of a non-Jewish background to adopt Jewish practices, such as circumcision. It was understandable that such new Christians should assume that they had to conform to a model of religious practice displayed by those who had brought them the good news of the gospel. Paul himself was circumcised, and was in the habit of worshipping in the synagogue. Even towards the end of his preaching life Paul felt it was necessary to visit the Temple in Jerusalem. Furthermore, it would have been known that Paul had circumcised Timothy, whose father had been a Greek. It would have seemed reasonable to follow this example. Paul, however, saw clearly that voluntarily adopting Jewish practices was an admission that the old covenant was still in force. A Jewish Christian might choose to observe the Law but it was essential at the same time to believe that Jesus Christ had brought into operation a more effective way of atoning for sin. For a non-Jew there was no point in adopting religious practices that had been made redundant.

The second strand running through Paul's letter is the justification of his own claim to have the authority to lay down rules on this or any other matter relating to the faith. Hence he devotes a great deal of the letter to a defence of his position and an account of the events which led to him having the responsibility for the non-Jewish Christians. We can assume that his opponents, if not actually members of those churches, were

---

[4]*Paul: A Critical Life*, Oxford University Press 1996, p. 162.

retailing accounts of Paul's dealings with the churches of Jerusalem and Antioch which showed him in a unfavourable light.

The traditional interpretation of Galatians has been heavily influenced by Luther's use of it to attack the Church of Rome. Luther was obsessed by this letter, and saw in it a perfect description of the conflict between living faith and dead works. 'The epistle to the Galatians is my epistle,' he said; 'I have betrothed myself to it: it is my wife.' Unfortunately, Luther's idiosyncratic interpretation was followed by many commentators, and there was (and still is) a widespread assumption that this letter's main theme is the contrast of justification by faith with justification by the performing of meritorious deeds, as though the Jews or, for that matter, Roman Catholics did not believe in justification by faith. It has been shown, however, by more recent commentators that the essential feature of Judaism was the covenant with God, not the earning of salvation by good works. Paul is attempting to show that Christians share in this covenant because of the sacrifice of Christ, and share in it more effectively. In other words, we are counted righteous or justified because of God's free gift, and we maintain our relationship with God by obedience or faith. We cannot earn God's favour simply by good works. This is true whether we are Jews or Christians. Paul is not attacking good works but the ritual observances of an outmoded covenant which has been superseded by a new and more effective covenant. So the theme of Galatians is not the superiority of faith to works, but the superiority of the new covenant, which involves faith in Christ, to the old, which involves faith in the Law of Moses. When Paul in this letter speaks of 'works', he nearly always defines them as 'works of the Law'. Indeed, he refers even more frequently simply to 'the Law'. J. D. G. Dunn[5] observes that commentators usually recognize that Paul only

---

[5] *Jesus, Paul and the Law*, SPCK 1990, p. 219.

uses the phrase 'works of the Law' in the context of his argument with other Jewish Christians or Jews, adding, 'But sooner or later (usually sooner) the perspective slips and the assumption begins to dominate the exegesis that by "works of the law" Paul means the attempt to win God's favour by human achievement, or some such paraphrase.'

The contrast between this letter and that written by another contemporary of Paul's, namely the writer of the Letter to the Hebrews, is striking. There is no doubt that Paul's audience are for the most part non-Jews. Paul's main purpose is to discourage non-Jews from adopting the practices of orthodox Judaism, whereas the writer to the Hebrews is clearly addressing Jews who had become Christians and were being tempted to return to Judaism. Hence the approach used is very different. Jews could only be persuaded in theological arguments by copious use of relevant texts from the scriptures, which is the main feature that distinguishes the Letter to the Hebrews. Paul does indeed use scriptural references and a rabbinical method of reasoning from them, but on the whole his approach is a more direct appeal to reason and common sense. This is not to say that there were no Jews amongst the churches of Galatia; that would be an absurd claim. But it is obvious that Paul is appealing to the Gentile members of the churches.

At the same time we should recognize that the two letters share a lot of common ground. The core argument of Galatians is the same as that of Hebrews, namely, the superiority of the new covenant of Christ to the old covenant of Moses. Furthermore, the position of Abraham in relation to the new covenant is virtually identical in both letters: those who share in the promises of Christ's covenant are inheritors of the promises made by God to Abraham. Christ is the means whereby we are accepted within the covenant, whereas those who cling to the Law of Moses, the old covenant, are rejecting God's grace which comes through the new covenant. This is why both Paul and the writer of the Letter to the Hebrews are anxious to establish the superiority of Abraham to Moses. In short, a Jew who has become a Christian has to be assured by the writer to the Hebrews that he is still a son of Abraham. On the other hand, a Gentile Christian who fears that he is not a true son of Abraham because he is not circumcised, has to be persuaded by Paul that his relation to Abraham is not impaired but actually strengthened by his faith in Christ.

Unlike other letters of Paul, which cover several issues, often a main theological argument together with matters of a general pastoral nature, this letter is devoted largely to one theme. It is also remarkable how frequently the author refers to himself.

It might be useful to give here a detailed plan of the structure of the letter.

1. *Introduction*
(1.1–5) Greetings.
(1.6–9) Paul accuses the Galatians of abandoning the original gospel due to the bad influence of others and condemns those responsible.

2. *Paul's defence* – an account of events relating to the issue
(1.10–24; 2.1–17) Paul's appointment as an apostle directly by God. Events in Jerusalem and Antioch and his relationship with the leaders of those churches.
(2.18–21) Paul feels that it is impossible for him to return to the Law because he is dead to the Law and only lives in Christ. If one can be justified by the Law Christ died for nothing.

3. *The main argument – Abraham and the Mosaic Law*

A. *Preliminary remarks*
(3.1–5) It is foolish to go back to the Law if you originally received the Spirit of God not from following the Law but from hearing the gospel of Christ.

B. *The promise given to Abraham*

(3.6–9) Abraham was justified by his faith in God, and the promise given by God to him that all the nations (i.e. the Gentiles) would be blessed in him applies to all who have faith.

(3.10–14) Those who trust in the Law are automatically condemned because of the text which states that those who do not follow all the precepts of the Law are under a curse. As no one is capable of performing all that the Law commands, nobody can escape condemnation. God states that the just shall live through faith. Christ took on this curse on our behalf so that the blessing given to Abraham might come into effect.

(3.15–18) This promise or covenant, which cannot be set aside, applies to Abraham 'and his seed'. His seed is Christ. The covenant given to Abraham pre-dates the covenant of Moses and still applies because it is not dependent on the later covenant which established the Law.

C. *The purpose of the Law*

(3.19–20) The Law is inferior to the promise given to Abraham because, firstly, it was a temporary measure to deal with sin and applied only until Christ appeared, and secondly, it was not given to the Jews directly from God but mediated through angels and Moses.

(3.21–25) Even so, the Law did not contradict the earlier promise; by defining sin it prepared the ground for the covenant of faith in Christ to come in. The Law acted as our minder until that time.

(3.26–29) You are all children of God through your baptism into Christ; you have put on Christ. You are all one and also inheritors of the promise given to Abraham because of your relationship with Christ.

(4.1–7) Our position before Christ came was that we were like children under guardians who have not yet taken up their inheritance. Children who have not reached the age of majority are like slaves. We were slaves to the elemental powers of the world. Now God has sent his Son, we have entered our inheritance and God has enabled us through the Spirit to call him 'Father'. We are no longer slaves.

D. *The absurdity of wanting to return to their former state*

(4.8–10) How can you want to be slaves again of those ineffectual elementary forces represented by the observance of a ritual calendar?

(4.11–20) I am afraid all my efforts on your behalf have been a waste of time. I became like you – why can't you become like me? You accepted me once, even though my illness caused you some inconvenience. Why have you turned against me? My opponents' motive is to exclude you so that you will want to chase after them. You should not have to have me there to keep you on the right lines. I am suffering again on your behalf. I wish I could be there now and try another approach because I am at a loss what to say.

4. *The second argument – the two children of Abraham*

(4.21–31) If you want the Law, hear the Law, for it says that Abraham had two sons, one by a slave, Hagar, and the other by a free woman, Sarah. These women stand for the two covenants: Hagar for the covenant given on Sinai which leads to slavery, and which is represented by the earthly Jerusalem, and Sarah for the heavenly Jerusalem, which is free. Just as Sarah's son Isaac was persecuted by Hagar's son Ishmael, so we are persecuted today. We are the children of the free Sarah, not the slave Hagar.

5. *How all this applies to you*

(5.1–6) Since Christ has given us freedom, do not give it up. If you are circumcised, you are obliged to perform all the requirements of the Law, and if you have recourse to the Law you lose the grace of Christ. It is irrelevant whether you are circumcised or not. What counts is faith working through love.

(5.7–10) You were making such progress. Those who have been influencing you are not acting for God. It only takes a few to ruin the rest, but I am sure you will not listen to them.

(5.11–12) Furthermore, if I am supposed to be advocating circumcision, why are they still attacking me? If I did advocate circumcision, I would be able to get rid of the one great obstacle which separates Jew from Christian, i.e. the crucifixion. I would rather get rid of the troublemakers.

(5.13–15) The freedom you have been given is not an excuse for self-indulgence. You are expected to serve others in love. Love is the whole Law. Bickering amongst yourselves will destroy you.

(5.16–26) Follow the spirit, not the flesh. They are opposed to one another. If you are governed by the spirit, you are free from the Law. If you commit the works of the flesh, you will not inherit the kingdom of God. Those who belong to Christ have crucified the flesh. Let us not be self-centred or malicious to one another.

6. *Final pastoral advice*

(6.1–10) Check those going astray. Carry one another's burdens. Don't think too much of yourselves. Don't rely on others for financial support. Share your wealth with those teaching you the faith. You will be judged. Those who follow the flesh will be punished, those who follow the spirit will gain eternal life. Do good to everybody, particularly fellow Christians.

7. *Signing off*

(6.11–18) I am writing this with my own hand: those who are advocating circumcision are motivated by a desire for self-preservation and by insincerity. They want to boast about the numbers in their party. All I boast about is the cross of Jesus. The true Israelites who follow Jesus will be blessed. I have been marked by the stripes of Christ and so ask for your respect. Grace be with you.

Before you start – a few things to note

1. The text of the letter is my own. I have attempted to keep close to the original. This should enable the reader to pick out

individual words or phrases more easily, although it does make for a more wooden rendering.

2. Certain abbreviations will appear throughout. They are as follows:

AV	Authorized Version
NT	New Testament
NEB	New English Bible
OT	Old Testament
Sept.	Septuagint
Vulg.	Vulgate (the Latin version of the Bible by St Jerome)

3. The commentary will follow the text, which will be given in small extracts. This should make it easier to use when studying individual passages on their own or when time is limited.

4. So much has been written on the letter to the Galatians that it would be impossible to list everybody who has contributed to the writing of this guide. I owe a great deal in particular to the great nineteenth-century scholar Bishop Lightfoot whose commentary is listed along with other authors whose works I have consulted during the course of working on Galatians. I have also referred to the original commentaries of Chrysostom and Jerome. A bibliography of more recent works can be found at the end of this book. I append here a list of most of the ancient writers I have referred to, together with some much abbreviated biographies, in the hope that they will be of interest to readers.

Biographies

Augustine (354–430) Bishop of Hippo in north Africa, who was converted to Christianity from Manichaeism and whose most famous works are his *Confessions* and *The City of God*.

Wrote a commentary on Galatians around 394. (Lightfoot, while acknowledging Augustine's excellence as an interpreter of scripture, regards the commentary as inferior, observing that 'spiritual insight, though a far diviner gift than the critical faculty, will not supply its place'.)

Celsus Platonist pagan philosopher who wrote around 180 a book called 'True Word' in which he attacked Christianity. Origen replied with a work entitled 'Against Celsus'.

Eusebius (around 260–340) Probably a native of Palestine. Survived the persecutions of 303–310 and later became Bishop of Caesarea. Present at Council of Nicaea. Prolific writer most famous for his *History of the Church*.

John Chrysostom, 'Golden-mouth' (around 349–407) Wrote a commentary on Galatians while still in Antioch. Became bishop of Constantinople, famous for his preaching. Died in exile after offending the empress Eudoxia.

Clement of Alexandria (around 150–215) His writing on Christian subjects was heavily influenced by the humanism of pagan Greek literature. Head of the Catechetical School in Alexandria until the outbreak of persecution under Septimius Severus forced him to leave Alexandria.

Clement of Rome (died around 100) Third or fourth bishop of Rome and reputedly a disciple of Paul and Peter. Wrote at least one letter to the Corinthians. The second letter to the Corinthians attributed to him is most probably by a later writer.

Ignatius, 'Godbearer' (died around 108) Third bishop of Antioch, who was sent to Rome to be martyred. On his journey he wrote seven letters to various churches.

Jerome (around 345–420) Studied in Rome and spent some time in Constantinople with Gregory of Nazianzus. Settled in Bethlehem, where he founded four monastic communities. Attacked Pelagianism. Famous for his translation of the Bible into Latin. Around 387 wrote a commentary on Galatians which relied heavily on works of Origen now missing.

Josephus (born around 37) Pharisee who took part in the Jewish rebellion against the Romans. Captured in 67, he settled in Rome. Wrote *The Jewish War* and *Antiquities*. Although pro-Roman, he defended the Jewish race and religion against the Alexandrian scholar Apion.

Origen (around 185–254) Christian Platonist and biblical scholar. Wrote at least fifteen books and seven homilies on Galatians, none of which has survived. Taught first in Alexandria and then Palestine, where he was ordained priest. Imprisoned and tortured during Decian persecutions.

Philo (around 30 BC–AD 45) Head of Jewish community in Alexandria. Sent as delegate to Rome to ask emperor Caligula for exemption for Jews from duty of worshipping emperor. Combined Judaism with Greek philosophy, particularly Platonism. Prolific writer on subjects connected with scripture and theology.

Tertullian (around 160–225) Trained as a lawyer. Spent most of his life in Carthage. Most important for his ability to express Christian terms in Latin. Defended Christianity against pagans and Jews and expounded Christian doctrine and practice in the church. Later joined the strict Montanist sect.

Chapter 1

1 Paul, an apostle not from any human appointment nor through any human being, but through Jesus Christ and God the Father who raised him from the dead, 2 and all the brethren with me, [send greetings] to the churches of Galatia. 3 Grace to you and peace from God our Father and the Lord Jesus Christ 4 who gave himself for our sins, in order to rescue us from the present wicked age, according to the will of God our Father, 5 to whom [be] glory for ever and ever, amen.

[1, 2] The immediate issue for Paul is to establish his authority. It comes neither *from* human beings, **apo anthrôpôn**, nor *through* any human being, **dia anthrôpou**, but through God and his Son. The distinction between the two prepositions and between the singular 'man' and the plural 'men' is subtle. The origin of Paul's authority is not to be found in a group of people nor is his authority mediated to him through a single person. He was directly appointed as an apostle by God. The fact that 'Jesus Christ' is contrasted with 'man' shows that Paul regards him as more than a human being. Paul is establishing his credentials to speak with authority precisely because he feels that his credentials have been questioned. At the same time he makes the point that he is not on his own, but is supported by his fellow Christians, 'all the brethren with me'.

[3] 'Grace', **charis**, and 'peace', **eirênê**, are the components of Paul's greetings in all his letters. In those written to Timothy we find a third, 'mercy', **eleos**. **Charis** is not another form of the normal secular greeting, **chaire**, 'hail', although philologically related, but a particularly Christian salutation. Grace and peace are gifts of God. **Eirênê** is the Greek form of the Hebrew *shalom*.

Charis is a word of such richness that no translation can do it justice. One of its earliest uses is to denote outward grace or beauty. Then it is found in the sense of a grace or favour, either offered or felt. In other words, it is a kindness offered or the gratitude felt by the recipient. At the same time it can also describe joy or pleasure. In a religious context it can describe the state the righteous enjoys in the sight of God, i.e. approval. This is well established in the OT. For example, 'But Noah *found grace* in the eyes of the Lord', Gen. 6.8 (AV), **Nôe de heure charin enantion Kûriou tou Theou** (Sept.). In the NT the sense is frequently that of a free gift given not in return for a favour or as a reward for good behaviour but out of love. We might call this the core theological sense of the word in Paul, but at the same time we should be conscious of the word's other meanings. Hence in the greeting, 'Grace to you . . .', we should take it to mean, 'May God continue to give you his approval and at the same time pour blessing, joy and his gifts of love upon you.' (See also my note on Heb.12.28 in *Reading through Hebrews*.)

[4] '*For* (or *on behalf of*) our sins', **hyper tôn hamartiôn hêmôn**, Vulg. *pro peccatis nostris*, is the reading of several manuscripts, but there are other good manuscripts which give **peri**, a preposition normally translated as 'concerning' or 'about', but used elsewhere in the NT to mean the same as **hyper**. Although **hyper** tends to be used with persons and **peri** with things, in Heb. 5.1, 3 both prepositions are used with

'sins'; in v. 1 **hyper**, and in v. 3 **peri**, where the meaning is probably 'in regard to'. In verse 1 of this same passage in Hebrews **hyper** is also used with 'mankind', **anthrôpôn**, meaning 'on behalf of'. Paul uses the identical phrase **hyper tôn hamartiôn hêmôn** in I Cor. 15.3. Incidentally, the plural 'sins' in the Septuagint is always used in reference to the sin-offerings made on the Day of Atonement. At other times the singular tends to be used. It is significant that Paul and other NT writers such as the writer of Hebrews, by using the plural, are placing Christ's atoning sacrifice in the context of the yearly solemn festival of Yom Kippur.

'Rescue', **exelêtai**, rather than 'save'. The Greek verb means 'to take out of'.

'From the present wicked age', **ek tou aiônos tou enestôtos**, requires some comment. The word translated as 'age', **aiôn**, could also be translated as 'world', but it is likely that Paul has in his mind the notion of an era which is under the domination of a wicked power, which will be succeeded by an era ruled by Christ. Furthermore, to translate **aiôn** as 'world' might give the impression that he regarded the material world as evil. The description, 'present', indicates that he is thinking of a period of time. The concept is found in several forms in the NT. For example, Eph. 2.2 has 'the age of this world', **ton aiôna tou kosmou toutou**, but the commonest version, which occurs in the Gospels and is a favourite of Paul's, is 'this world', **ho aiôn houtos**. It is contrasted with 'that world', or 'the world to come', i.e. the eternal age of God's kingdom.

[5] There is no verb in this verse, so we can choose whether to make it a jussive, 'be', or, following the Vulg. *est*, a statement, 'is'.

'For ever and ever', **eis tous aiônas tôn aiônôn**, literally, 'into the ages of ages'. The use of the term **aiôn** picks up the reference in v. 4. This subtlety is missed in the English translation.

6 I am amazed that you are so quick to abandon the one who called you by [Christ's] grace and to change to another gospel. 7 Not that there is another gospel – except that there are some people upsetting you and wanting to pervert the gospel of Christ. 8 But even if we or an angel from heaven preach a gospel to you different from that which we have preached to you, let him be accursed. 9 As we have said before, and I say again now, if anyone is preaching to you a gospel different from the one you received, let him be accursed.

[6] Some commentators have used Paul's phrase, 'so quick', to argue that this letter must have been written soon after the second time he preached to the Galatians. This is reading too much into the phrase, since we can date the letter on other evidence to a period much later than this. **Houtôs tacheôs**, 'so quick(ly)', would only have to carry the sense 'so soon' if there were a clear reference to an earlier event *after* which the action of the verb qualified by **houtôs tacheôs** is taking place. Paul is not saying, 'You are abandoning God so soon after he has called you.' To say to a child, 'You are eating too quickly', is not the same as saying, 'You are eating too soon' 'You are eating too soon' would only make sense if it were followed by a phrase such as 'after your breakfast'. The Galatians are eager to change; they are not necessarily changing too soon.

'Abandon . . . change' is one verb in Greek, **metatithesthe**.

'The one who called you', as we can prove from other references in Paul's letters and elsewhere in this chapter (v. 15), is God. 'Christ's' is bracketed to draw attention to the fact that it does not appear in all the manuscripts, although there is a strong argument for including it here. **En chariti**, 'by grace', could possibly be translated 'into grace', as in the Vulgate version, *in gratiam*, but there is little advantage in doing so. We can also translate it as 'in grace'. The preposition **en** in classical Greek nearly always carries the meaning 'in', but by Paul's time was starting to convey the sense 'by' or 'with'. In Paul this usage is particularly common.

[7] This verse is best treated as an interruption to qualify the previous verse. The reference in v. 6 to 'another gospel', **heteron euangelion**, might have been taken by Paul's audience as suggesting that there was an alternative. **Heteros** is used when talking of one of two possibilities, hence it can also mean 'second' or 'different'. In this verse the word translated as 'another' is **allo**, the word used when speaking of more than two. In other words, there is no other gospel at all. The NEB 'Not that it is in fact another gospel' misses this point.

'Upsetting', **tarassontes**, 'disturbing' or 'causing disorder'; 'pervert', **metastrepsai**, 'alter' or 'twist around'.

[8, 9] 'Accursed', **anathema**. The literal meaning is 'an object declared taboo or dedicated to a god', hence devoted for destruction. This word is used in the Sept. to denote something handed over for destruction, e.g. Josh. 7 tells how the Israelites became **anathema** themselves when one of them stole objects which had been declared **anathema**. As a result they were defeated by the men of Ai. The curse was only removed when the guilty party together with the taboo objects and all his possessions and family were destroyed. In the early church this word and its cognate verb **anathematizein** gradually came to be used to denote the milder concept of excommunication.

10 Yes, for am I now in the business of persuading human beings or God? Or is it that I am seeking to please people? If I were still pleasing people I would not be Christ's servant. 11 For I want you to know,

brothers and sisters, that the gospel preached by me is not one based on human terms. 12 For I was not taught it, nor did I receive it from a human being, but through a revelation of Jesus Christ.

[10] This verse is to be understood as an explanation of Paul's strong words in the previous verse. His unpopular stance is due to the fact that he would rather please God than people. As Lightfoot puts it, 'Let him be accursed, I say. What, does my boldness startle you?' The language is rather obscure for a reason characteristic of Paul's style, namely his tendency when emotionally stressed to let his thought swamp his language. We need to supply the steps he has left out of his argument.

The first question can be paraphrased, 'Do you think I need to persuade God? Don't be ridiculous! It's *you* I am trying to get through to.' The same thought occurs in the first part of II Cor. 5.11, 'So knowing the fear of the Lord, we are persuading men, but we have been revealed to God (i.e. God knows me already).' Paul would say in answer to his own rhetorical question, 'I *am* in the business of persuading people – that's my job. But there is no point in persuading God – he already knows me inside out.' The second rhetorical question can be paraphrased, 'Or perhaps you think I am interested in being popular? Come off it! If I wanted to be popular, I would not be serving Christ.'

Lightfoot interprets the first part of this verse differently, and portrays Paul as arguing, 'You charge me with a policy of conciliation. Yes; I conciliate God.' In other words, Lightfoot misses the point of the rhetorical question by treating the questions as though they are genuine inquiries. Consequently he seems to think that Paul *is* trying to persuade God.

[11] 'Based on human terms', **kata anthrôpon**, literally, 'according to man'. The gospel Paul preached was **kata theon**, i.e. divine or superhuman.

[12] 'Through a revelation', **di' apokalypseôs**, refers either to the appearance of Christ to Paul on the Damascus road, or to a revelation of the truth of the gospel by Christ at that time. Whether we should take it to be a revelation *of* Christ, i.e. an appearance of Christ, or a revelation *by* Christ of something else, is difficult to decide. One should also remember that Christ appeared to Ananias 'in a vision', **en horâmati** (Acts 9.10), and confirmed Paul's appointment as an apostle. This could be described as a revelation both *of* and *by* Christ. In v. 2 of the next chapter we can see **apokalypsis** used in the sense of 'explanation'.

13 For you heard how I once adhered to the Jewish way of life, and used to persecute to an extreme the church of God and wreak havoc on it, 14 and how I outstripped in my orthodoxy many contemporaries amongst my people, being excessively devoted to my ancestors' traditions. 15 But when God, who ordained me from my mother's womb and called me through his grace, saw fit 16 to reveal his son through me so that I should proclaim his gospel among the Gentiles, I did not immediately consult flesh and blood 17 or go up to Jerusalem to those who were apostles before me, but went away into Arabia and turned back again to Damascus.

[13] 'You heard' (no doubt from Paul himself on the occasion when they first met) 'how I once adhered to the Jewish way of life', **tên emên anastrophên pote en tôi Ioudaïsmôi**, literally, 'my way of life once in Judaism'.

'Wreak havoc', literally, 'lay waste'. This verb is repeated in v. 23.

[14] 'Outstripped', **proëkopton**, from a verb meaning literally 'to cut one's way forward', a military term for the action of a pioneer. See the note on 5.7.

'Orthodoxy', literally, 'Judaism'; 'devoted', **zêlôtês**, a word also applied to the extreme partisans who fought the Romans. See note on 4.17.

'Ancestors' traditions' are probably not just the Mosaic laws but the whole body of religious doctrine and practice associated with the Pharisees.

[15] This verse is reminiscent of Jer. 1.5 (Sept.), 'Before I formed you in the belly I knew you and before you came out of the womb I sanctified you, and appointed you as a prophet for the nations' (Isa. 49.5, though similar, would probably have been taken by Paul as a Messianic prophecy). Since the word in the Jeremiah passage translated as 'nations', **ethnê**, also means 'Gentiles', we can see why Paul would regard this text as particularly applicable to himself.

'Ordained' is closer than the AV 'separated' to the Greek **aphorisâs**. The verb **aphorizô** here carries the sense of a spiritual setting apart or appointing for a special purpose, rather than a physical segregation, which is the meaning it conveys when it is used in 2.12 to describe Peter's withdrawing himself from the company of Gentile Christians at meals. The Vulgate *qui me segregavit de utero matris meae* seems to imply a physical separation.

'Called', **kalesâs**, literally, 'having called', cannot be taken as implying that he had already been converted to Christianity some time before he became aware of his ordination as an apostle. The call and the consciousness of his special ministry came at the same time. Paul's conviction that he had a special mission is referred to in Rom. 1.1, 'Paul, a slave of Christ Jesus, called (**klêtos**) as an apostle, set apart (**aphôrismenos**) for the gospel of God'. Note that the same verbs occur, i.e. **kaleô** and **aphorizô**.

[16] 'To reveal', **apokalypsai**, picks up **di'apokalypseôs** in v. 12. See Acts 9.15–17. It should not be taken, however, as a reference to Paul's vision of Christ, i.e. 'to reveal *to* me', but rather the revealing of Christ to the Gentiles (and others) by Paul's preaching. '*To* me' cannot be correct for **en emoi**, which must mean '*by*, *with*, *in* me', hence, '*through* me'.

'I did not consult', **ou prosanethemên**, from the verb **prosanatithemai**, which in classical writers frequently carries the sense of consulting an expert, such as an interpreter of dreams or an oracle, rather than the sense of conferring or discussing with a colleague.

[17] Acts does not mention Paul's visit to Arabia, and immediately after describing his escape over the wall of Damascus speaks of his visit to Jerusalem with Barnabas (Acts 9.25–27). It is easy to see significance in this omission, but the account in Acts is not a neat chronology or log-book of everything that happened to the apostles. Whether this reference to Arabia means that Paul visited Sinai, as Lightfoot suggests, or merely lay low in the desert outside Damascus, is impossible to know. Nor can we say how long Paul stayed in Arabia.

Early Christian scholars such as Jerome and Chrysostom thought that Paul preached while he was in Arabia. Jerome also treats the reference to Arabia as an allegory of the Old Testament. In other words, his going away into Arabia signifies that Paul searched for Christ in the scriptures. When he had found him there, his return to Damascus is represented as a return to the 'blood and suffering of Christ'. Chrysostom sees Paul's mission to Arabia as following upon the need to preach the gospel everywhere and praises Paul's fervour and commitment in undertaking the instruction 'of wild and barbarous men'.

18 Then after three years, I did go up to Jerusalem to

visit Cephas and I stayed with him fifteen days. 19 I did not see any other apostle except James the Lord's brother. 20 Look here, before God, what I am writing to you is no lie. 21 Then I went to the area around Syria and Cilicia. 22 I was personally unknown to the Christian churches in Judaea. 23 They were merely hearing that their former persecutor was now preaching the faith on which he had once wreaked havoc, 24 and they glorified God in me.

[18] The visit to Jerusalem must be the one described in Acts 9.26–29. Paul does not say that he only stayed two weeks in Jerusalem, but that he stayed two weeks with Peter. From Acts we can see that he spent some time travelling in and out of Jerusalem. The visit to the Temple to which Paul refers in Acts 22.17 probably occurred at this time.

'To visit', **historêsai**, '[a word] used by those who are looking at great and famous cities', according to Chrysostom. We could also translate it as 'to get to know'. The Vulgate has *videre*, 'to see'. In classical Greek the word meant 'to inquire' and is related to the noun **historiâ**, 'an inquiry', from which we derive 'history'. It probably indicates that Paul visited Peter for the purpose of asking him questions. It would be odd if he had not a great deal to ask him. As C. H. Dodd drily comments, 'We may presume they did not spend all the time talking about the weather.' At the same time, the meaning 'to visit' is well-established in contemporary Greek.

Chrysostom and Jerome do not see Paul's visit to Peter as the homage paid by an inferior to his superior. Chrysostom makes the point that Paul was **isotîmos**, i.e. 'of equal honour', with Peter, and that he needed nothing from him. His visit to him was a courtesy shown to someone who was 'more important and older', **meizona kai presbyteron**. Jerome says that Paul went to Jerusalem *non tam disciturus aliquid ab apostolis,* *quam cum eis evangelium quod docuerat collaturus*, 'not so much to learn something from the apostles, as to discuss with them the gospel he had taught'. He goes on to say that Paul's purpose in visiting Peter was 'not to look at his eyes, cheeks and face, to see whether he was lean or plump, whether he had a hooked or a straight nose, whether hair covered his brow or he was bald-headed, . . . not through eagerness to learn, because he himself had the same sponsor for preaching (i.e. Christ), but to show honour to the first apostle'.

'Cephas', the Aramaic form of 'Peter', i.e. 'Rocky', a nickname given to Simon by Jesus, is most commonly used by Paul. In the next chapter, however, he uses 'Peter'.

[19] Acts 9.27 speaks of Barnabas introducing him to the apostles. We are not told who they are, and so there is no justification for seeing a discrepancy either between Acts and Paul's statement here that he only met Peter and James, or in the fact that Paul does not mention Barnabas. Paul seems to include James among the apostles in I Cor. 15.7 when he states that the risen Christ was 'seen by James then all the apostles'. There is no rigid definition of the term 'apostle', which is certainly not restricted to the Twelve.

'James the Lord's brother' requires some comment because the precise meaning of 'brother' has been a bone of contention among scholars. Was James: (a) the son of Mary and Joseph, (b) the son of Joseph by an earlier wife, (c) a cousin of Jesus? Origen, commenting on John 2.12, speaks of the brothers of Jesus, i.e. James and Judas, as sons of Joseph 'by a wife who had died beforehand', and again in another passage associates this view with those 'who wish to preserve the honour of Mary in virginity throughout'. He seems to share this view himself, since he adds, 'and I think it reasonable that as Jesus was the first-fruit of purity and chastity among men, so Mary was among women: for it is not seemly to ascribe the first-fruit of virginity to any other woman but her'. Clement of Alexandria also supports Origen. It is significant that Jesus on the cross entrusted his mother to John (John 19.26–27), not James or Judas. If Mary had other children still living one would have thought that there would have been no need to give someone else the task of looking after her. Tertullian, however, apparently believed that the Lord's brothers were the later children of Mary and Joseph. This notion was attacked by Jerome, who took the view that both Mary and Joseph were virgins, in a treatise written around 383 contradicting the views of Helvidius who had agreed with Tertullian. Jerome's argument was that 'brothers' denoted a looser relationship, i.e. Judas and James were cousins of Jesus. Just as in Gen. 13.8 Abraham had referred to his nephew Lot and himself as 'brothers' (Sept. **adelphoi**), and again in Gen. 29.15 Laban calls his sister's son Jacob 'brother', **adelphos**, so the title of brothers when applied to the Lord's brethren was, according to Jerome, not to be taken literally. The strongest argument against Jerome is that the vast majority of Christian writers before his period did not interpret the word 'brother' in this way and it was not until the end of the fourth century that his view started to become generally accepted in the church. Those interested in investigating this matter in more detail are referred to the chapter on 'The Brethren of the Lord' in Lighfoot's commentary.

[20] Why is Paul so concerned to emphasize that he only saw Peter and James, and that he only went to Jerusalem after a three year interval? Clearly because his enemies were saying that: (a) he had been appointed by the church in Jerusalem and therefore was subordinate to them; (b) he had been heavily influenced by the Jerusalem leaders in formulating his method of preaching the gospel and its content. Paul insists that he was appointed directly by God.

[21] This verse does not contradict the statement in Acts 9.30

that the brethren took him to Caesarea (the port on the coast of Palestine, not Caesarea Philippi, the inland town north of Galilee) and sent him off to Tarsus. Tarsus is in Cilicia. We need not speculate whether Paul went directly to Tarsus or visited Syria on the way.

'The area around Syria and Cilicia', **ta klimata tês Syriâs kai tês Kilikiâs,** is an interesting expression. **Klimata** originally meant 'slopes', but became a technical term to describe the seven latitudinal strips into which the known inhabited world was divided by geographers. They marked the length of the longest day in half-hourly intervals, ranging from thirteen to sixteen hours. Syria and Cilicia are frequently mentioned together, and can be regarded as Paul's home ground.

[22, 23] 'Personally', literally, 'by face', **tôi prosôpôi.** Paul is not denying that he had been known personally by them in his previous role as persecutor, but making the point that after his conversion he was not seen by the Judaean Christians due to his activities in Syria and Cilicia. There is no discrepancy between Luke's statement that he was with the apostles going in and out of Jerusalem or disputing with the Hellenist Jews (Acts 9.28–29), and Paul's statement that he did not meet the members of the churches in Judaea.

'Christian', literally, 'in Christ'.

[24] A useful comment by Chrysostom, if anyone thinks Paul is lacking modesty. 'He did not say, "they marvelled at me, they praised me, they were amazed at me", but he showed that everything is of grace: "they glorified God in me".'

Chapter 2

1 Later, after an interval of fourteen years, I went up again to Jerusalem with Barnabas, taking Titus along with me as well. 2 I went there to give an explanation, and I laid before them the gospel which I preach amongst Gentiles, but [I did this] privately and before the important men, in case I was labouring or had laboured in vain.

[1] In spite of the various objections raised by commentators, this visit to Jerusalem seems to correspond with the visit described in Acts 15. Not only do many of the minor details fit, such as the fact that Paul was accompanied by Barnabas, but the special purpose of the visit and its outcome present a striking parallel with Luke's account. Paul does not mention his earlier mission bringing aid to the Christians in Judaea, which is noted in Acts 11.30, because (a) it was to the churches in Judaea and not necessarily Jerusalem; (b) it was nothing to do with the issue under discussion here. Luke does not mention Titus, probably because he was a minor figure at the time. Paul does mention him because his presence as an uncircumcised Christian provides significant evidence of Paul's stance regarding the circumcision of Gentiles. The date of this conference is around 51.

[2] 'To give an explanation', **kata apokalypsin**, literally, 'in

relation to disclosure'. 'To make a presentation' might be a more contemporary rendering. Some commentators who are convinced that this visit is the one referred to in Acts 11 see a connection with this phrase and the statement in Acts 11.28, 'One of them, called Agabus, stood up and declared through the Spirit that there would be a great famine over the whole world; and this occurred during the reign of Claudius.' As a result, they translate the phrase here as 'according to a revelation'. The NEB, for instance, has 'because it had been revealed by God that I should do so'. Even Lightfoot, who correctly states that the visit of Paul is not the one referred to in Acts 11 but is the conference described in Acts 15, takes the phrase in this sense. **Kata** can mean 'according to', 'following', or 'in accordance with', but it can also mean 'for the purpose of' or 'on the business of'. Nor is it necessary to take **apokalypsis** as a reference to some divine revelation; it merely means 'disclosure', and its cognate verb **apokalyptô** is often used to denote the revealing of an intention or motive. Incidentally, neither **apokalypsis** nor **apokalyptô** is used by Luke in the Acts 11.28 passage referring to Agabus' revelation. If Paul had intended the supernatural meaning, he would surely have added some explanation of the phrase. We must remember that we have the advantage of knowing Luke's account of the previous aid-bearing visit which was the result of Agabus' prophecy. Paul's Galatian audience were not likely to have been thinking of this earlier visit, and would therefore not automatically interpret the phrase **kata apokalypsin** in a supernatural sense.

'I laid before', **anethemên**, or 'I imparted', not 'I consulted', which would be **prosanethemên**. See the note on 1.16. The use of the verb **anatithemai** does not imply an inferiority in the person who was doing the imparting. Acts 25.14 uses the same verb to describe the procurator Festus laying Paul's case before king Agrippa. It would be a bold man who suggested that Festus was a subordinate or in any way inferior to Agrippa. It is clear from the context that Paul had a clear notion of what his policy was and was simply informing the church leaders in Jerusalem about it. At the same time he was asking for their approval. That is clear from the clause, 'in case I was labouring (literally, 'running') or had laboured in vain'. The matter was probably the most important one to be discussed in the early church and could have split the church in two if it had not been handled sensitively. It is easy to see how this conference could have been described by Paul's enemies; they would have claimed that he was a man humbly begging pardon for his actions and seeking enlightenment from his superiors.

'I preach', **kêryssô**, literally, 'I proclaim'. The noun cognate with this verb is **kêrygma**.

'Privately and before the important men' does not contradict the account in Acts. There is no need to follow W. F. Knox, who claimed, 'Any identification (of Paul's account) with Acts 15 implies that one of the two accounts is a hopeless falsification: one describes a strictly private meeting of the leaders of the church, the other a public meeting of the whole.' This argument is based on a wrong assumption. According to Luke, there were two meetings, the first one being held to welcome Paul and Barnabas and to hear the general news of their work, and the second the one attended only by the apostles and elders. Paul is clearly referring not to the preliminary meeting (15.4), where the Pharisaic party amongst the members present advocated circumcision, but to the committee meeting that immediately followed this (15.6).

'The important men', **tois dokousin**, does not carry any derogatory sense, such as 'those who were thought of as important'. The phrase **hoi dokountes** simply means 'those of repute', or 'men of authority'. Paul picks up the phrase later and qualifies it (v. 6), but it is not in itself a derogatory term.

3 But even so, Titus, a Greek who was with me, was

not forced to accept circumcision. 4 Because of the false brethren who had been allowed in on the side, who had inserted themselves to spy out the freedom which we have in Christ Jesus, so that they might enslave us, 5 we did not give in to them even temporarily by subordinating ourselves, so that the truth of the gospel should remain as it was in regard to you.

[3] 'But even so . . . not', **all' oude**, literally, 'but not even', should be taken as qualifying Paul's previous admission that he was seeking approval for the way he dealt with Gentile Christians: '*even* though I was allowing that I could have been taking the wrong line, I *still* would *not* have Titus circumcised.' The case of Timothy, who was circumcised by Paul, occurs to mind. Why was Paul reluctant to allow Titus to be circumcised? Because the two cases are entirely different. Timothy, whose father was a Gentile, had a Jewish mother and so by rabbinic law was Jewish, and Paul wished to use Timothy specifically in his work in Jewish communities. There is evidence that Timothy continued to work with Jewish churches from the reference to him in Hebrews 13.23. Acts 16.1–4 makes it quite clear that Paul wished to give Timothy proper credentials for entering and speaking in the synagogue. There was no intention to use Titus for this work since he was from a non-Jewish background.

It has been suggested by those who interpret the words 'was not *forced* to accept circumcision' as implying that Titus *voluntarily* undertook the operation. We are to imagine, I suppose, that Paul said to Titus, 'Well, here we are in Jerusalem. How about having you circumcised? It will look well on your c.v., and impress the apostles.' The suggestion that Paul, who at the time was arguing against the circumcision of Gentile Christians, should allow such a thing to happen, is most unconvincing.

[4, 5] A tortuous syntax, usually a sign of deep emotion in Paul, makes these verses difficult to unravel. 'Because of', **dia**, is not the preposition one would expect. Why not 'despite' or something similar? But there is a logical connection; Paul is giving the *reason* for his subsequent actions: '*because of* these people who would have used any excuse to re-impose the Mosaic law, I was determined to dig my heels in and not make any concessions which they could have twisted to their purposes.'

'The false brethren who had been allowed in on the side', **tous pareisaktous pseudadelphous. Pareisaktos**, 'Substitute-on-the-Side', was, according to Strabo (*Geography*, XVII, 794), the nickname of Ptolemy XI, father of the famous Cleopatra, also called the 'Flute Player', who reigned in Egypt 80–51 BC. He was so called because he had been allowed into the dynasty in order to marry another Cleopatra who was descended from a concubine of Ptolemy VIII, whose line was consequently by-passed. It is clear from this description that Paul suspects that these people, who are undermining all his work with non-Jewish Christians, are some sort of fifth column acting for a reactionary Jewish group, most probably those very Pharisees whose cause he had previously supported, and whose opposition is described in Acts 15.5.

'Not . . . even', **oude**, is omitted by one or two manuscripts but is found in all the best ones.

Têi hypotagêi, 'by subordinating ourselves' or 'by adopting a submissive role'.

6 But from the important men – (what they once were makes no difference to me; God makes no distinction when it comes to a human being) – well, the important men added no further requirements in my case. 7 On the contrary, seeing that I had been entrusted with the gospel of non-circumcision as Peter was with the one

of circumcision, 8 for he, who had worked through
Peter in the mission of circumcision, had also worked
through me in regard to the Gentiles, 9 and knowing
the grace given to me, James, Cephas and John, who
were regarded as authorities, gave Barnabas and me
the hand of fellowship, so that we [should deal] with
the Gentiles and they [should deal] with the circumcised. 10 [The] only [stipulation was] that we
should remember the poor, and that was the very thing
I had been eager to do.

In the original, the whole of the above passage is, syntactically
speaking, one sentence. The omissions, sudden changes of
direction, the condensed arguments, the interruptions and
asides make it difficult to follow. As a result it is helpful
occasionally to attempt to expand the text.

[6] '*From* the important men' would lead us to expect a
phrase such as 'came no further demand', but, changing his
grammar in mid-sentence, he continues as though he had
started the sentence with 'The important men . . .'

'Makes no distinction', **prosôpon ou lambanei**, literally,
'does not take the face', from a Hebrew expression which could
be rendered 'to accept the face', i.e. to approve of. In the NT
prosôpon lambanô always has a bad sense, that of partiality or
of being impressed by externals, such as wealth or status.

'Added no further requirements', **ouden prosanethento**,
from the same verb **prosanatithemai** used above in 1.16 to
mean 'to consult'. This is its basic meaning, 'to put on someone
an extra (burden)'.

Paul's statement that the apostles added no further requirements seems at first sight to contradict the statement in Acts

15.20, 29 that the Gentile Christians were required to avoid meat offered to idols, blood, meat from strangled animals and fornication. There is no discrepancy when we recall that the issue which Paul is discussing in the letter to the Galatians is circumcision. Therefore, the statement 'added no further requirements' should be taken as though it were immediately followed by a clause such as 'to what had already been accepted'.

The particular dietary laws mentioned above had most probably already been accepted by the Galatians and it is likely that Paul had advocated such prohibitions at the very start of his ministry. It was only later when the church spread to a more pagan environment like Corinth that these dietary laws would be questioned. As to fornication, we may assume that the Galatians already knew that it was unacceptable. Even so, Paul still feels it necessary to remind them of its unacceptability (5.19).

[7] Tertullian (*On the Prescribing of Heretics*, 23) comments on the division of tasks between Peter and Paul that it was so that each might preach not a different gospel but to a different audience; they had divided their tasks, not the gospel, *inter se distributionem officii ordinaverunt, non separationem evangelii, nec ut aliud alter sed ut aliis alter praedicarent*. In fact, as we know, they both preached to Jews and Gentiles alike. The statement that Paul had been entrusted with the gospel to the uncircumcised and Peter with that to the circumcised is not a rigid demarcation but a recognition of their separate core responsibilities.

[8] 'He who had worked through Peter', **ho energêsâs Petrôi**, is God. **Energeô** has a whole range of meanings, some of them medical. For instance, the surgeon who operates is described as **ho energôn**, the patient being operated on as **ho energoumenos**. The verb also means 'to be efficacious' (e.g. a drug), or 'to be

effective'. The word 'energy', while philologically related, has a different connotation. The same is true of the word **dynamis**, which tends to be associated with 'dynamite'. One is advised to be wary of obvious associations when referring to the Greek of the original text.

[9] 'James' is not the son of Zebedee who was martyred around 44, but 'the Lord's brother' mentioned above (1.19). As James the son of Zebedee was no longer alive at the time of this conference, there is no longer any need to differentiate between them by adding the phrase 'the Lord's brother'. There is a third James, the son of Alphaeus, but it is unnecessary to differentiate this James from him, since his position in the church was less important.

'Regarded as authorities', **hoi dokountes stûloi einai**, literally, 'those appearing to be pillars', i.e. regarded as pillars. The metaphor occurs in classical Greek but is also a Jewish one used in particular to describe great teachers. Clement of Rome (I Clement 5.2) refers to Peter and Paul as 'the greatest and most righteous **stûloi**'.

'Fellowship', **koinôniâs**, Vulg. *societatis*. They shook hands as a token of their agreement, not a gesture common among the Jews but one particularly respected among the Persians.

[10] 'Remember the poor': Paul had proved his concern for the poor by his previous mission bringing aid to the needy in Judaea, as described in Acts 11.29–30. It has also been suggested that 'the poor' is an epithet by which the church in Jerusalem was commonly known and that 'remember' has some meaning like 'acknowledge their merits'. It is unlikely that the second of these suggestions can be accepted, but the first certainly seems to carry some weight. The Qumran literature frequently uses the term 'the poor', *Ebionim*, as a way of referring to the members of that community and it is tempting to see a parallel with the use of the term here and even

a connection between the two groups. When the Judaizing Christians split from the main body of the church and formed a distinctive sect, did they join the Qumran community? Certainly they were referred to as 'the Ebionites' according to Eusebius (*History of the Church*, III, 27). Leaving aside this interesting question, we can be sure that the term 'the poor' also carries a clear message that the church in Jerusalem and the surrounding area needed material aid from Christians in more prosperous communities.

11 But when Cephas came to Antioch, I personally stood up to him, because he had been criticized. 12 For before certain people had come from James, he used to eat with the Gentiles. But when they came, he began to withdraw and separate himself in respect for the circumcised. 13 And the rest of the Jews pretended to agree with him, so that Barnabas also went along with their pretence. 14 But when I saw that were not being straight with the truth of the gospel, I said to Cephas in front of everybody, 'If you, a Jew, can live like a Gentile and not like a Jew, how can you force Gentiles to live like Jews?

[11] Calvin and Luther were not slow to use this incident to prove that Peter, and by association the Pope of Rome, could err. Earlier theologians saw in it a proof of Peter's humility. Origen, and later Jerome, found the incident so embarrassing that they claimed the two leaders were pretending to disagree and acting out some elaborate charade, a view attacked by Augustine. Clement of Alexandria even said that it was a different Cephas.

'Criticized', **kategnôsmenos**, rather than 'condemned', which would imply that some sort of judgment had been passed on Peter. This verb is frequently used in the sense of 'to lay a charge against someone'. The Vulgate translates **kategnôsmenos** as *reprehensibilis,* which must mean '*fit* to be criticized'. Because he is anxious to prove that Paul was not really quarrelling with Peter, Jerome states that it was not Paul who found fault with Peter but the members of the church with whom Peter used to eat and whom he was now avoiding.

[12] The 'certain people' who had come from James could not be Judas and Silas. They were already in Antioch, having accompanied Paul and Barnabas back to the city (Acts 15.27–34) to support Paul's stance. Silas accompanied Paul on his next mission after Paul had fallen out with Barnabas.

The reason why the issue of dietary laws had cropped up again was because the matter had not been comprehensively defined in the first place. One can see why Peter was placed in a quandary. The conference in Jerusalem had set the ground rules for the Gentiles, but nothing had been established regarding the dietary laws applying to the Jewish Christians in Antioch. In fact, according to the account Luke gives in Acts, the original letter sent by James had only been addressed to the Gentiles (Acts 15.23). The question of relations between Jewish and non-Jewish members, especially in regard to eating together, seems to have been left in the air. Peter had clearly assumed at the start of his visit to Antioch that there was no problem in his eating together with Gentiles. We need not assume that the new objections made by the people who had come from James were in contradiction of the final agreement reached at the conference in Jerusalem. It simply had not occurred to anyone beforehand to ask the question, 'And what about those occasions when Jews and non-Jews are eating together?' For James and Peter the separation of Jew from Gentile at meal times was probably not as crucial as it was for Paul. Murphy-O'Connor (*Paul: A Critical Life,* p. 152) suggests that James 'did not see it as at all incongruous. In fact he must have been surprised and offended by Paul's reaction.'

There has been speculation that the issue was to do with additional observances such as hand-washing or special prayers. Some have suggested that tithing was one of the points causing disagreement. There is no evidence for this, and Paul would surely have mentioned it if the visitors from Jerusalem had been trying to introduce observances which had not been specified at the conference. This whole incident underlines the problem involved in allowing Jewish Christians to keep their old dietary laws. It was impossible to have a church where one group could not eat with the other. Either the Jews gave way or the Gentiles adopted the complete Judaic dietary regime. The issue of observance of the Mosaic Law eventually split the church and gave rise to the Ebionites, who preserved the traditions of Judaism. Incidentally, the Ebionites later used this incident for a veiled attack on Paul.

[13] 'Pretended to agree', **synypekrithêsan**, implies that Barnabas and the other Jewish Christians of the church in Antioch did not wholeheartedly approve of what Peter was doing.

[14] 'Being straight', literally, 'walking upright', from **orthopodeô**, a verb not found before Paul uses it in this passage. It is possible to take it in the sense of 'to advance, make progress', but such a sense is not appropriate here.

Paul's argument is rather condensed in this verse: he is saying that Peter is in effect putting moral pressure on the non-Jews to adopt Jewish practices, by abandoning his policy of living like a Gentile. Peter is also being inconsistent in that, having previously shown the Gentiles that a Jew such as he is can live a non-Jewish life, he now seems to be denying this.

15 We are Jews by nature and not Gentile sinners, 16

but we know that a human being is not justified by the works of the Law without faith in Jesus Christ, and we believed in Christ Jesus so that we might be justified by faith in Christ and not by the works of the Law, because no flesh will be justified by the works of the Law. 17 If, while seeking to be justified by Christ, we were found to be sinners ourselves, [was] Christ a servant of sin? God forbid!'

[15] 'We are Jews by nature', **hêmeis physei Ioudaioi**, refers to the fact that Paul and Peter were born and bred as Jews.

'Gentile sinners', **ex ethnôn hamartôloi**, literally, 'sinners from the nations', is a tautology. Gentiles are often defined as 'sinners', and the two terms seem to be interchangeable. Because they do not observe the Law, they are automatically **hamartôloi**. This can be shown by comparing two different versions of Jesus' preaching on the subject of loving those who love you. In Matt. 5.47 we read, 'surely even the Gentiles (**ethnikoi**) do the same?' In Luke 6.33 we have, 'even the sinners (**hamartôloi**) do the same'. Paul deliberately and ironically uses both terms because the whole burden of his argument is that (a) we are all sinners, Jews and non-Jews alike; (b) the Law cannot take away sin.

[16] We now reach the main core of Paul's theme with the first mention in this letter of the word 'Law'. There can be little doubt that this is the *Torah*, which is translated as **nomos** in Greek. Unfortunately, both Greek and English fail to convey the full sense of 'Torah'. The Hebrew word means 'teaching' or 'instruction' and is used in a variety of ways. Firstly, it means the Pentateuch, the first five books of the Bible; secondly, it means the Mosaic Law and everything to do with it, such as the rabbinic teaching about the Law; and thirdly, it stands for all Jewish religious teaching and literature.

'By the works of the Law', **ex ergôn nomou**, means the observances which are associated with the *Torah*, such as circumcision, rituals of sacrifice and fasting, dietary practices, etc. Note that Paul is not consistent in his use of the definite article. 'The Law' is frequently referred to simply as 'Law'. In this verse the definite articles are omitted before both 'works' and 'Law'. It is important to note this habit of omitting the definite article, since it is too easy to jump to the conclusion that Paul is speaking of all observances of a legal nature, i.e. any acts performed to conform with a code of law. His message cannot be taken as an attack on the concept of a moral code or formula. Finally, it should be kept in mind that Paul never refers in this letter to the plural 'works' on their own – they are followed six times by 'of the Law', and once, in a different context, by 'of the flesh'.

The second important word which Paul now introduces to us for the first time in this letter is 'justified'. It might be useful at this point to look at **dikaioô**, 'to justify', together with the abstract noun formed from the verb, **dikaiôsis**, 'justification'. The verb was used in classical writers to mean, among other things, 'I set right', 'I pronounce judgment on', 'I do justice to', hence 'I punish' (and its converse), 'I acquit'. In the Sept. and the NT it takes on the sense of 'I pronounce (or 'treat as') righteous', 'I vindicate'. So 'justification' is 'making (or 'accounting') righteous'. For Paul, justification is always to do with forgiving sinners, whereas in the OT it is associated with rewarding or vindicating those who have not broken the Law. There is no need to make a strict distinction between '*making* righteous' and '*treating* as righteous'. If God treats the sinner as righteous, then, for all practical purposes, he *is* righteous. If his sins are wiped out, he is **dikaios**, 'just' or 'righteous'. Hence for Paul justification involves sanctification, and he does not hesitate to call his Christian brethren **hagioi**, 'holy' or 'saints'. As he says in I Cor. 6.11, 'And such were some of you (i.e. sinners); but you have been washed, *you have been sanctified*, **hêgiasthête**, *you have been justified*, **edikaiôthête**.'

'Without faith', literally, 'if not through faith', **ean mê dia pisteôs**, is preferable to '*but only through* faith' (NEB), which might be what we would have expected Paul to have said. He seems, however, to be making a more subtle point, namely, that as long as one has faith in Christ, following Jewish traditions does no harm. It is attempting to seek justification through these practices that is wrong.

Because 'in Jesus Christ' (and later in this verse 'in Christ'), literally translated, can mean '*of* Jesus Christ', some have suggested that it refers to the faith (i.e. faithfulness) shown by Christ, and not to the faith of the believer in Christ. But here, and in 3.22 where the same phrase occurs, the way in which the verb 'believe', **pisteuô**, is also used seems to indicate that the faith is the believer's, not Christ's. Because Paul uses the verb 'we believed', **episteusamen**, in this verse, it is natural to assume that the faith of which he speaks is faith in Christ.To put it in grammatical terms, it is more likely that 'of Jesus Christ' is an objective, not a subjective genitive. This was the traditional view amongst commentators.

On the other hand, it has been more recently argued that the reference to the believer serves to demonstrate that the believer's *faith in Christ* is a response to the *faithfulness of Christ*. As Murphy-O'Connor puts it (*Paul: A Critical Life*, p. 204), 'the faith/fidelity of Christ is evoked, not in and for itself, but because it is both the cause and exemplar of the faith/fidelity of Christians. Their active commitment is both enabled by, and modelled on, that of Christ.' While admitting the doctrinal attraction of this argument, I suggest that the only way to decide whether the phrase **pistis Christou** should be translated as 'faith in Christ' (objective) or 'faith[fulness] of Christ' (subjective) is to examine cases where **pistis** is found followed by other nouns in the genitive in the NT generally

and in Paul's letters in particular. A quick survey gives the
following:

1. **'of' cases (subjective):** 'the faith of Abraham', Rom.
4.12; 4.16; 'the faith[fulness] of God', Rom.3.3; 'your
faith', i.e. 'the faith of you' (very frequent), e.g. Rom. 1.8;
Matt. 9.22, 29; 15.28; Mark 5.34; 10.52; Luke 8.25, 48; I
Thess. 1.8; 3.2, 5, etc. (common in this letter).

2. **'in' cases (objective):** 'faith in his name', Acts 3.16; 'faith
in being saved', Acts 14.9; 'faith in God', Mark 11.22.

We find for the most part that when the genitive following
pistis can definitely be translated as 'of' (i.e. subjective), the
genitive overwhelmingly tends to be one of the personal
pronouns, 'our', 'your', 'their' etc. Other subjective genitives
seem to be extremely rare. When we look for examples of **pistis**
followed by 'of Christ/Jesus', we can find eight cases (twice in
Romans, three times in Galatians, once in Philippians, once in
James and once in Revelation). We do, however, also find **pistis**
followed by **en**, 'in', and then 'Christ/Jesus', e.g. Gal. 3.26;
Eph. 1.15; Col. 1.4; I Tim. 1.14, 3.13; II Tim. 1.13, 3.15; and
occasionally by **eis** or **pros**, 'towards', e.g. Acts 20.21; 24.24;
Col. 2.5; Philemon 1.5. In other words, these are cases which
must be translated by 'in'. It is reasonable to assume that cases
where **pistis** is followed by the genitive of 'Christ/Jesus' are
synonymous with cases where **pistis** is followed by **en**, **eis** or
pros. The context in which they occur is the same. In short, they
are objective genitives. In conclusion, there is no example
where we can state categorically that **pistis Christou** must
mean 'faith[fulness] of Christ'.

'No flesh will be justified' is suggested by Ps. 143.2 (AV),
'for in thy sight shall no man living be justified'.

[17] The interpretation of this verse is difficult, but it helps if
we recall that 'sinners', **hamartôloi,** is also a synonym for
'Gentiles'.

Is Paul saying, 'If, in order to obtain justification by Christ, we return to the Law and so become sinners like the Gentiles, is Christ responsible for bringing us into sin?' Remove the rhetorical question and this now becomes, 'If we have to return to observing the Law in order to be justified by Christ, Christ would actually be serving as an agent of sin.' Is this what Paul is saying? The difficulty with this interpretation is that it supposes that Paul is speaking of the consequences of returning *in the future* to the observance of the Law, whereas it is clear from the tense of 'we were found' that he is speaking *of the past*. The better way to take the verse is to assume that it refers to the original conversion of Paul and Peter to Christ. To paraphrase, Paul is saying, 'If, in order to obtain justification by Christ, *we abandoned the Law* and *became* sinners, i.e. Gentiles, *was* Christ responsible for bringing us into sin?' To put it another way, 'When we became Christians and abandoned the Law as a means of justification, we placed ourselves outside the Law and became like the Gentiles, i.e. sinners. Did that make Christ the agent for sin? Is he guilty of making us sinners? Of course not!'

The problem is caused by Paul's condensed argument, the irony implicit in the reference to **hamartôloi,** and the lack of a main verb. He assumes that his audience will take this verse in the context of following the observances of the law. This is made clear by the next verse which refers to building up what he has broken down, i.e. returning to the Law. But why would returning to the Law inevitably make one a sinner? Because all who try to follow the Law fall short of perfection. Trying to be justified by the works of the Law automatically carries with it failure and hence sin.

Some might take the verse literally and argue that Paul is simply saying, 'If, in the course of trying to live a Christian life, we commit a sin, Christ cannot be held responsible.' That might be true, but it is not relevant to this argument.

I have assumed that this is the last part of Paul's address to

Peter, because in the next verse he changes from 'we' to 'I' and seems to be addressing the Galatians directly. It is possible, however, to argue that the break occurs at the end of the chapter.

18 For if I build up again what I have broken down, I make myself a law-breaker. 19 For I, through the law, have died to the law, in order to live to God. I have been crucified along with Christ. 20 I am no longer alive but Christ lives in me, and the life I live in the flesh, I live in the faith of God's son, who loved me and gave himself up for me. 21 I do not reject the grace of God, for if righteousness [comes] through the Law, then Christ was killed for nothing.

[18] 'Law-breaker', or 'transgressor', **parabatên**.

[19] This is a complex sentence, again because the thought is condensed. Paul is saying that it was through the Law that sin came and hence death, a theme he develops more fully in Romans. Without the Law he would not know sin or death (Rom. 7.9–11, 'I once lived without the Law, but when the commandment arrived, sin came alive and I died, and the commandment that was meant for life, was found in me to be for death; for sin, taking hold through the commandment, cheated me and killed me through it.') The Law was necessary in order for him to know sin and so to die, in order to be resurrected with Christ. Christ was killed by crucifixion and hence Paul shared this symbolically in baptism, when he died to sin and rose to life.

[20] 'In me', **en emoi**, which can also be translated as '*by* me'. Both prepositions are appropriate: in one sense, Christians are

only truly alive because Christ lives in them; in another sense, Christ is embodied and made manifest in the world by living in the bodies of his disciples.

En pistei, 'in (or by) the faith'. Again there is a double meaning: Paul's life is lived *in* faith; as Lightfoot says, 'the atmosphere as it were which he breathes in this his new spiritual life', or *by* faith, that is, the means by which he lives and the new Law which rules his life.

'Of God's son'; either the faith is given to the believer by God's son or it is the faith of the believer in God's son. If we believe it is the latter, we could translate the phrase as '*in* God's son'. As for interpreting the phrase as referring to the faithfulness *shown by* God's son, see the notes on v. 16 above.

'For me', **hyper emou**; another preposition with more than one meaning. This phrase can mean 'instead of me', 'as a substitute for me', or 'on my behalf', or even, 'on account of me'.

'Gave himself up', i.e. 'surrendered' rather than simply 'gave', from **paradidômi**.

[21] The argument is a little obscure: Paul seems to be saying, 'In rejecting the Law, I am not rejecting the grace of God; if the Law is still to be followed, Christ's death was unnecessary and irrelevant.' He is answering a hypothetical, or perhaps an actual, objection from the Judaizing party, namely, that to reject the *Torah* is to reject the bounty of God. Paul would counter this with the question, 'If the *Torah* is still in force, what is the point of Christ's sacrifice?'

'Righteousness', **dikaiosynê**, clearly interchangeable with **dikaiôsis**, 'justification'. See note on v. 16 above.

'For nothing', **dôreân**, literally, 'gratuitously, as a gift'.

Chapter 3

1 You senseless Galatians! Who has bewitched you, you before whose eyes Jesus Christ was openly depicted on the cross? 2 All I want to know from you is this – did you receive the Spirit from the works of the Law or from a response to faith? 3 Are you so senseless as to begin with the Spirit and finish up now with the flesh? 4 Did you suffer so much to no purpose, if it was indeed to no purpose?

[1] 'Bewitched', **ebaskanen**, usually by the evil eye. This is clearly alluded to by the reference in the next part of the sentence, 'before whose eyes'. The blessings given to them by seeing Christ on the cross are contrasted with the curse of seeing a malign agent. To look into the eyes of a witch allows the evil influence to enter one's soul. Lightfoot quotes (unfortunately without translating) from a passage attributed to the scientist Alexander Aphrodisiensis (third century AD), who says (*Problems* 2, 53), 'They discharge from their pupils, as it were, a poisonous and destructive ray, and this, entering through the eyes of the person to whom they bear malice, will overthrow his soul and nature.'

'Openly depicted', **proegraphê**, a verb used to denote posting up a public notice or advertisement.

[2] 'Receive the Spirit' is a reference to the gift of the Spirit to those who have accepted the gospel of Christ.

'From a response to faith', **ex akoês pisteôs**, literally, 'from hearing faith'. Is this 'hearing about the faith', or 'hearing and believing'? Lightfoot suggests 'hearing that comes of faith'. There is a similar phrase in Rom. 1.5 and 16.26, **eis hypakoên pisteôs**, translated in the AV as 'for obedience to the faith' and 'for the obedience of faith' respectively. If **akoê** here is a synonym for **hypakoê**, it denotes the response of the faithful and obedient believer. On the other hand, it could be a reference to hearing the good news, and be similar to the phrase **logos akoês**, 'the word of hearing', i.e. the report one hears. I Thess. 2.13 is relevant here, 'when you received *from us the word of God we had heard* (**logon akoês par'hêmôn tou Theou**), you welcomed it not as a human message but as God's message . . .' So it is possible to translate **ex akoês pisteôs** as 'from hearing about [the gospel of] faith'. The Romans passages referred to above could also be understood in this sense, if conversely we can take **hypakoê** as a synonym for **akoê**. See also my notes on Heb. 4.2 in *Reading through Hebrews*. Whichever translation we prefer, the main point is clear – the works of the Law are being contrasted with faith.

[3] The words translated here as 'begin' and 'finish' are both found in the context of religious ceremonies, 'begin', **enarchomai**, being used in pagan rites to refer to the first act of taking the barley from the basket and **epiteleô** being used to mean 'discharge (a religious duty)', 'pay in full (tribute)', or 'celebrate'. Paul uses the similar word **proenarchomai** together with **epiteleô** in II Cor. 8.6, and the identical pair of words **enarchomai** and **epiteleô** in Phil. 1.6, the latter of which is particularly relevant: 'trusting in this very thing, namely, that *he who began* (**ho enarxamenos**) in you a good work, *will perfect it* (**epitelesei**) until the day of Christ Jesus.'

[4] The only historical evidence for the sufferings referred to in this verse is that found in Acts 14, which describes the persecution of the Gentile Christians in Iconium and Lystra. It has been suggested that the Greek verb **epathete**, 'you suffered', can be taken in the sense of 'you experienced'. Hence, 'Did you enjoy so many good experiences . . .?' This use, however, is unknown in the NT, where the verb always conveys the sense of suffering. Paul frequently refers to the suffering that converts to Christ will endure. Acts 14.22 is particularly apt. After being stoned by the Jews outside Lystra, Paul together with his fellow evangelists went on to preach in the area: 'strengthening the resolve of the disciples and encouraging them to remain firm in the faith, and telling them that *it was through many troubles that we must enter the kingdom of God.*'

'To no purpose', **eikêi**, or 'in vain', 'pointlessly'. The meaning of the conditional clause, 'if it was indeed to no purpose', is not immediately apparent. It must be understood as implying that Paul is correcting what could be seen as an admission by him that the Galatians were beyond redemption. He hopes it was not going to be a waste of time – he expects better of them.

5 So, does he who supplies you with the Spirit and who works acts of power in you, [come] from the works of the Law or from a response to faith? 6 As Abraham had faith in God, and that was put down to him as righteousness, 7 know then that those [who come] from faith are sons of Abraham. 8 The scripture, foreseeing that God justifies the Gentiles from faith, gave Abraham a preview of the gospel in the words, 'all the nations will be blessed in you'. 9 So those [who come] from faith are blessed along with faithful Abraham.

[5] 'He who supplies', **ho epichorêgôn**, a word which conveys the sense of generous giving and providing. It is especially used in contemporary papyri to describe a husband's provision for his wife.

'Who works acts of power', **energôn dynameis**. See above, note on 2.8. The root of the noun **dynamis** is **dynamai**, 'I can'. So **dynamis** is the ability to perform something out of the ordinary, not necessarily a display of strength and might. 'Miracle' as a translation of **dynamis** can also be misleading, since it tends to be used to describe a phenomenon which violates natural law, rather than denote a manifestation of the power of the Creator in his creation. The powers conferred by the Holy Spirit do not always have to be spectacular.

'In you', **en hûmîn**, or 'by you'.

There is no main verb in this sentence. 'Come' goes with 'from' fairly well, but 'is' would be the usual addendum. We could also have made it a past tense, 'did come' rather than 'does come'.

[6] The argument of this and the next verses is also found and developed in Romans 4. In brief, it was important for Paul to establish the following points:

1. Abraham is the father of all Christians, not just Jewish Christians.
2. Abraham is righteous, i.e. saved, by faith, not by performing some act of religious observance such as circumcision.
3. The promises made by God to Abraham are fulfilled in the gospel of Christ.
4. All those who have faith in Christ share the blessings conferred on Abraham.

The reason why Abraham is a key figure in Paul's theology, and indeed in the theology of other writers such as the author of the Letter to the Hebrews, is because the Judaizers would have used the texts referring to Abraham against the Gentile Christians. For example, Gen. 17.10 (AV), 'This is my covenant, which ye shall keep, between me and you and thy seed after thee; every man child among you shall be circumcised.' Paul would counter this with such texts as Gen. 22.16–18, 'By myself have I sworn, saith the Lord, for because thou hast done this thing, and hast not withheld thy son, thine only son: that in blessing I will bless thee, and in multiplying I will multiply thy seed as the stars of the heaven, and as the sand which is upon the sea shore; and thy seed shall possess the gate of his enemies; and in thy seed shall all the nations of the earth be blessed; because thou hast obeyed my voice.'

Abraham was a favourite subject of those interpreters who relied on allegory to extract deeper meanings out of the text. For instance, to Philo (*On Abraham*, 68–70), Abraham's move from Chaldaea stands for the abandoning of a belief in astrology. To the rabbis the change of his name from Abram to Abraham, and that of his wife from Sarai to Sarah, was highly significant, because God had added the letter H to both names, the same letter that occurs twice in God's own name YHWH (D. Goldstein, *Jewish Legends*, p.50). Philo (*On the Changing of Names*, 76), following a particularly intricate and tortuous line of reasoning, sees Abraham's change of name as signifying the change from the study of nature to moral philosophy and the abandonment of the contemplation of the **kosmos** for the acquiring of knowledge of the *creator* of the **kosmos**.

This verse is an almost exact copy of the Septuagint version of Gen. 15.6, **kai episteusen Abr[a]âm tôi Theôi, kai elogisthê autôi eis dikaiosynên**, a text which is quoted again in Rom. 4.3. Here, instead of **kai episteusen Abraâm**, we have **kathôs Abraâm episteusen**, and in Romans, **episteusen de Abraâm**. The minor discrepancies would indicate that Paul is quoting from memory a familiar text from the Greek version of the scriptures. The significance of the text is clear when one looks at the passage in which it occurs. God has just promised

Abraham that his seed will be as numerous as the stars in heaven, and Abraham immediately 'believed'. This faith in God was sufficient for Abraham to be justified – 'it was put down to him for righteousness'. This faith in God is the simple response to God's promise, and is a model for all those who are justified by faith.

[7] Just as Abraham's faithful response to God resulted in his justification, so those who exhibit the same faith are the sons of Abraham and also are justified.

[8] This verse is a fusion of two texts in Genesis: 12.3 (Sept.), 'and all the *tribes* (**phûlai**) of the earth will be blessed in *you*', and 18.18, 'and all the *nations* (**ethnê**) of the earth will be blessed in *him*'. Paul has taken 'in you' from 12.3 and 'nations' from 18.18, while omitting 'of the earth' altogether.

'Gave a preview of the gospel', **proeuêngelisato**, literally, 'gave good news beforehand'. This links the promise given to Abraham with its fulfilment by Christ.

[9] This verse rounds off the argument: the faith shown by Abraham is the same as the faith shown by the Christian believer, so the Christian shares the same blessing as that given to Abraham.

It is worth pointing out that **pistis** and its cognate adjective **pistos** have a wider sense than any word we can find to translate them. Basically, **pistis** is both intellectual 'belief' and emotional 'trust' or 'obedience'. It is also active 'trustfulness' and passive 'trustworthiness'. The same variety of meanings attaches to **pistos**, which means 'faithful' or 'trustworthy'. Regarding this subject, see the notes on 11.6 in *Reading through Hebrews* and, for a fuller account of the different ways in which these concepts are handled in Latin, Greek and Hebrew, pp. 154–8 of Lightfoot's commentary.

10 All those who are of the works of the Law are under a curse, for it is written that everyone who does not abide by all the things written in the book of the Law and do them is accursed. 11 It is clear that no one is justified by the Law in God's view, because 'the just through faith shall live'. 12 And the Law is not of faith but 'he who has done them shall live by them'.

[10] 'Of the works of the Law', **ex ergôn nomou**, i.e. 'relying on' or 'based on'.

The standard interpretation of this verse is that all who rely on the Law for justification are in fact doomed because it is impossible for any human being to keep *all* the commandments of the Mosaic Law; there will always be something one neglects to do or some sin that one inevitably commits. Because the Sept. version of Deut.27.26 says '*every* one who does not abide by *all* the words of this Law to do them is accursed', it follows that all who rely on the Law are under this curse. Incidentally, Jerome noticed that the Hebrew version of this verse did not have 'every' or 'all', and unfairly concluded that the Jews had deliberately altered the text.

There is, however, a second interpretation which suggests that Paul's argument is that those who put their trust in the performance of the works of the Law are under a curse because they are missing the main point of the Law, which is to rely on God's mercy and to love one's neighbour as oneself. Following Paul's statement in 5.14 that the whole Law is summed up in one sentence, 'you shall love your neighbour as yourself', this alternative interpretation claims that anyone who thinks it sufficient to possess membership of the covenant and to perform the rituals involved in that membership is not displaying a real understanding of God's grace or a real faith in God. His justification is invalid not because he has missed out

some ritual or broken an individual commandment, but
because he has the wrong attitude to God and is not living by
faith.

The latter interpretation is very plausible. and at the same
time theologically attractive, but it might lead us to the
conclusion that Paul thought it was possible to be justified by
the Law by adopting a more spiritual attitude towards its
observances or by following its core commandments. Paul,
however, frequently argues that the Law is in itself an obstacle
to faith. In Romans 4, a passage which has many similarities
with this chapter in its argument regarding Abraham's
justification by faith, Paul argues (vv. 13,14) that the promise
made to Abraham did not operate through the Law (**dia tou
nomou**) but through the righteousness of faith (**dia dikaiosynês
pisteôs**), and adds: 'For if those relying on the Law (**hoi ek
nomou**) are heirs, faith is made void and the promise is
nullified.' Again in Rom. 7.8 Paul says, 'Without the Law sin is
dead.' Although Paul is always careful to avoid saying that the
Law is in itself evil (see Rom. 7.12, 'the Law is holy and the
commandment holy, righteous and good') and clearly accepts
that it has a special purpose in moral evolution, he seems to see
the Law as hindering the operation of God's grace and as being
in opposition to faith. We should therefore be cautious about
accepting the notion that the curse comes into effect only when
the inner purpose of the Law is not understood. As Lightfoot
observes, 'Supposing the fulfilment of the law possible, still the
spirit of the law is antagonistic to faith.'

As further evidence that the first interpretation is the more
likely, we might consider the point made by Jesus in the Temple
(John 7.19) when he said to his opponents, 'Didn't Moses give
you the Law? Yet none of you carries out the Law.' In other
words, it is impossible to perform all that the Law requires. Yet
the same passage can be interpreted differently since it goes on
to describe how Jesus takes the case of circumcision, which his
opponents could perform on the sabbath, and compares it with

his own act of healing which he also had performed on a sabbath. He says (vv. 23, 24), 'Are you angry with me because I have made the whole of a man healthy on the sabbath? Don't judge *according to appearance* (**kat'opsin**, literally, 'according to sight') but make a righteous judgment.' This passage could lend support to the second interpretation, i.e. the proper performance of the Law lies in carrying out the underlying purpose of the Law, not its individual commandments.

Although the former of the two interpretations is to be preferred, we can see that there is no great gulf between them, nor should we reject the second one out of hand. Paul would agree that the underlying purpose of the Law is love (Rom. 13.10, 'Love is the fulfilment of the Law') and would probably also concede that those who claim to observe the Law are under the curse because they are missing the real point of the Law. But we must not obscure his main argument, i.e. that the Law gets in the way of a proper relationship with God, since it has been made redundant by the new covenant which is activated and which only operates through faith in Christ.

[11] 'In God's view', **para tôi Theôi**, literally, 'in the presence of God'.

'The just through faith shall live', not the more usual 'the just shall live through faith', which is ambiguous and could be taken as saying simply that the righteous person should live his life in a trusting way. Paul is actually saying that it is only the person who is justified by faith who will live, i.e. inherit eternal life. This quotation from Habakkuk 2.4 is also found in Romans 1.17, where again the context makes it clear that only those justified by faith will be saved from the wrath of God.

[12] Paul uses this verse, which quotes from Lev.18.5, to imply that the Law does not involve faith, since to be justified by the Law one has simply to carry out its commandments. In other words, the Law defines the righteous as those who *do* all

the Law requires. The devout Jew might argue with Paul that the Law does involve faith, the faithfulness of the obedient servant, but Paul's point is that the emphasis in the Leviticus passage is on the actual performance of the Law's commandments and not on the faith of the performer.

13 Christ redeemed us from the curse of the Law by becoming a curse for us, as it is written, 'Cursed be everyone who is hanged on the gallows', 14 in order that Abraham's blessing might come about for the Gentiles by Christ Jesus, so that we might take up the offer of the Spirit through faith.

[13] 'Redeemed', **exêgorasen**, 'bought up' or 'bought out'.

'Us' has been taken by some commentators as referring to Paul and his fellow Jews, but this passage clearly applies to all Christians, Jewish and Gentile alike. The Law was a curse to the Gentiles because it excluded them from the covenant and defined them as sinners, and it was a curse to the Jews because, as v. 10 indicates, all those who attempted to observe the Law were accursed since they could not fulfil the Law's requirements.

The thinking behind the notion that Christ destroyed the curse of the Law by putting himself under a curse is not easy to follow. Paul does not tell us how Christ's sacrifice worked through his subjection to a curse but simply that it did work. All we can say is that Paul visualizes the curse which should fall on us as being transferred to the innocent Christ. The context is that of the scapegoat's role on the Day of Atonement. The quotation from Deut. 21.23 (with minor differences from the Septuagint version) refers to the prohibition against allowing the body of a executed criminal to remain on the gallows (literally 'timber', **xylon**, which can also be translated as 'cross') because the curse attached to the body would in some way pollute the land if the corpse was left unburied. Jewish interpreters faced with the numerous cases of Jewish patriots crucified by the Romans could not accept that those who had been executed were cursed by God. Consequently they interpreted the Deuteronomy passage as meaning that the hanged person was a reproach or an insult to God. In other words the curse applies to those who did the hanging.

[14] 'Take up the offer' rather than 'receive the promise', because the blessing is activated by Christ's sacrifice and the promise of the Spirit is not merely received as a future gift but fulfilled in the present **dia pisteôs**, 'through faith'. **Epangeliâ**, 'offer' or 'promise', is also used in a medical context to denote the curative property claimed for a drug, i.e. its beneficial effect. To put it another way, the Gentiles had 'received the promise' at the time Abraham was blessed, but they were able to 'take up the offer' and receive the Spirit when Christ's sacrifice was complete. **Epangeliâ** is a particularly appropriate term because it is used to denote a free offer rather than a pledge agreed on by two parties. It is used eight times in this chapter. While the promise in this passage is described by Paul as the promise of the Spirit, as it is in Acts 2.33, it is also the promise of eternal life, as we can see elsewhere in the NT such as I Tim. 4.8, 'of the now and the future life', and Heb. 9.15, 'of their eternal inheritance'.

15 Brothers and sisters, speaking from the human point of view, no one sets aside or adds a codicil to even a human covenant once it has been ratified. 16 The offers were made to Abraham and his seed – it does not say, 'and [your] seeds', as though it applied to many, but 'and your seed', meaning one, that is, Christ. 17 This is what I am saying: a covenant ratified beforehand by God is not rendered invalid by the Law

which came into being 430 years later, nor is the promise cancelled.

[15] The point of this verse is that the covenant, **diathêkê** (a word which also means 'will' or 'testament'), between God and Abraham is still valid, because even a human will cannot be set aside.

'Speaking from the human point of view', **kata anthrôpon legô**, literally, 'I speak according to a human being'.

'Adds a codicil', **epidiatassetai**, a legal expression only found in this passage. It is analogous to **epidiathêkê**, a word used by Josephus (*Antiquities*, XVII, 226) to mean 'an additional will' or 'codicil'.

[16] One might argue that it is a legal quibble to press the meaning of the singular 'seed' so far, but it is typical of rabbinical argument to extract as much significance as possible from the actual wording of scripture. Paul emphasizes the singularity of 'seed' because it is important to establish that the blessing of God is mediated through one person, i.e. Christ, to all Abraham's descendants and is not bestowed directly on them.

'The offers' are plural because God made more than one promise to Abraham. In Gen. 12.1–7 God promises that Abraham will found a great nation in a new land and in Gen. 17.4–6 he promises that Abraham will be the father of many nations. The writer of Hebrews also uses the plural when referring to God's promises to Abraham (Heb. 11.17).

[17] Paul repeats his argument because it was essential that his audience should understand that the original promise given to Abraham was not superseded by the Mosaic Law.

Some manuscripts add 'in(to) Christ', **eis Christon**, after 'by God', but this phrase is not found in the best manuscripts.

The interval of 430 years between the promise to Abraham and the creation of the Mosaic Law is taken from Ex. 12.40, where it refers to the length of time spent by the Israelites in Egypt. Gen. 15.13 refers to a period of 400 years during which the descendants of Abraham would be afflicted in a foreign land, but we can account for the discrepancy by arguing that either Gen. 15.13 is giving a round figure or Ex. 12.40 includes the sojourn of the patriarchs in Canaan before the migration. It is interesting that the Sept. version of Ex. 12.40 adds 'and in the land of Canaan' after 'in the land of Egypt'.

18 For if the inheritance [comes] from the Law, it [can] no longer [come] from the promise; but God has granted it to Abraham through a promise. 19 So what about the Law? It was added because of transgressions, until such a time as the seed to whom the promise applied should come, and it was drawn up by means of angels at the hand of a mediator. 20 The mediator is not [used] when there is one party, but God is one.

[18] For the addition of 'come(s)' see the note on 3.5.

'The inheritance' is the blessing given to Abraham and his descendants.

'Has granted', **kecharistai**, from **charizomai**, 'give freely', i.e. not in return for anything but as an act of grace. Hence **charis** is the noun we translate as 'grace'.

[19] 'So what about the Law?', literally, 'Why (or 'what') then the Law?'

'Because of transgressions', **tôn parabaseôn charin**, literally, 'thanks to trespasses', can be interpreted as meaning something like 'in order to define sin'. Can it also mean 'in order to check

or prevent sin'? From other passages in Paul's writings we can
see that he saw the primary function of the Law as providing
knowledge of sin and hence enabling the gift of grace to
operate. Compare Rom. 5.20, 'the Law came in so that sin
might be in excess; and where sin was in excess, grace was
super-abundant', and Rom. 7.7, 'I would not have known sin
except through the Law'. At the same time, as we can see from
vv. 22–25 of this chapter, Paul speaks of the Law as protecting
and guarding human beings until the time that Christ came and
presumably helping to prevent them from sinning. The Law
had a function but a temporary one. It has been superseded
because 'the seed to whom the promise applied', i.e. Christ, has
come.

'It was drawn up', **diatageis**, literally, 'having been drawn
up', from **diatassô**, 'I draw up' or 'I dispose', a verb which
applies to the disposition of troops and also to the drawing up
of a will or covenant. See above the note on **epidiatassetai** (v.
15).

'*By means of* angels', **di'angelôn**, not '*by* angels', because
they only assisted Moses. Although the OT only mentions the
angels' presence at the giving of the Law in Deut. 33.2, the final
part of which verse reads in the Sept. 'on his right hand the
angels with him', the angels who attended Moses are very
important in rabbinical thought. Josephus (*Antiquities*, XV,
136) speaks of the Jews as having learned 'the finest and the
holiest of the decrees in the laws from God *through angels*
(**di'angelôn**)'. It has been argued, however, that the word
angelôn in the Josephus passage actually should be translated
as 'messengers' and taken as referring to the prophets. D.
Goldstein (*Jewish Legends*, p. 98) repeats a traditional account
of how the angels were at first reluctant to allow Moses to
take the Torah away from heaven. He managed to persuade
them that mankind needed the Law more than they did. 'It is
written in the Torah, he said, "I am the Lord who brought
you out of the land of Egypt." Were you enslaved in Egypt? It

is also written "Honour your father and mother." Do you have parents that you need such a commandment? It is also written "Thou shalt not commit adultery." Are there any women in heaven that you need a prohibition like this?'

'At the hand of a mediator' seems to produce a Pavlovian reaction amongst commentators. Many, but not all, of the early Christian writers identified the mediator with Christ, probably because Christ is referred to by the writer of Hebrews three times as the mediator of the new covenant and I Tim. 2.5 speaks of Christ Jesus as the one mediator between God and men. It is obvious, however, that the mediator referred to here must be Moses. The references in Hebrews actually support this interpretation because Christ, by being called the mediator of the new covenant, is by implication being contrasted with Moses, the mediator of the old covenant. Paul is interested in a different argument because he is contrasting the non-mediated and direct promise of God to Abraham which has been fulfilled by the sacrifice of Christ with the mediated Law which is handed down to the Jews via Moses. This concept of Moses as standing between God and mankind is developed by Paul in II Cor. 3.12–16, where the fact that Moses put a veil over his face and a veil is worn when reading the Old Testament is contrasted with the direct approach made possible by the new dispensation.

[20] Lightfoot says of this verse, 'The number of interpretations of this passage is said to mount up to 250 or 300.' Fortunately, since many of these interpretations rest on the premiss that the mediator of the previous verse is Christ we can discount those. Any remaining difficulty is due to the abbreviated form of Paul's expression which, translated literally, goes, 'The mediator is not of one, but God is one.' 'The mediator is not of one' means 'the mediator is not used when there is only one person acting'. 'God is one' should be taken as

the minor premiss of a syllogism (whose conclusion we have to supply) which in its full form can be expressed as follows:

1. Mediators are not used when only one person is acting.
2. God is the one person acting in his dealings with Abraham.
3. Therefore there is no mediator used in God's dealings with Abraham.

In other words a mediator is used to negotiate between two parties who are acting and re-acting in a proposal. Where it is a one-way process, there is no mediation involved. God's promise to Abraham was an unconditional free gift, not an agreement between two parties. Furthermore, when God acts directly he does not need an intermediary. The Law of Moses was based on a conditional agreement between the Israelites and God. In Exodus 19 (vv. 3–8) we read how God told Moses to say to the people that *if* they would keep his covenant they would be 'a kingdom of priests, and an holy nation'. Moses approached the people with God's offer and 'all the people answered together, and said, All that the Lord hath spoken we will do' (AV). Moses then returned to God with their acceptance.

21 So the Law is against the promises of God? God forbid! For if the law that had been given had been capable of giving life, righteousness really would have come from the Law. 22 But the scripture enclosed everything under sin, so that the promise [coming] from faith in Jesus Christ should be given to those who believe. 23 Before faith came we were hemmed in and guarded under the Law pending the faith which was to be revealed. 24 So the Law became our minder for Christ, so that we might be justified through faith. 25 Since faith has come we are no longer under a minder.

[21] 'If the law that had been given had been capable of giving life', literally, 'If there was given a law which was able to make alive'. This life is clearly the spiritual life which is the fruit of the Spirit operating through faith. For Paul the spiritual life which the believer enjoys now is inseparable from the glorified life of the future kingdom. The interesting point is the connection with righteousness, **dikaiosynê**. Because the Law cannot make one righteous, **dikaios**, it cannot give eternal life either. Conversely, because it cannot 'make alive', **zôiöpoiêsai**, i.e. **poiein zôiön**, it cannot make one righteous. The conditional works both ways.

[22] 'The scripture' is singular, **hê graphê**, which usually means a particular passage in scripture rather than scripture in general, which is normally expressed by the use of the plural, **hai graphai**. We would therefore expect a quotation at this point. It is possible that the passage referred to is Deut. 27.26, quoted above in v. 10. Psalm 143.2, 'for in thy sight shall no man living be justified' (AV), quoted in 2.16, has also been suggested but it is hard to see that either verse is particularly relevant. It is more likely that 'the scripture' here is the Mosaic Law, i.e. those passages of scripture which contain the commandments of the old covenant, and which provided a comprehensive definition of sin and the remedies against it.

'Enclosed', **synekleisen**, 'fenced in', 'confined'. The Law, as Lightfoot puts it, 'subjected (the Jews) to the dominion of sin without means of escape'. But is this a fair picture? Enclosing and fencing in is as much a protective act as it is an imprisonment. Paul is probably contrasting the restrictions of the old covenant with the liberty of the Christian believer. The confinement under the Law was a necessary part of mankind's evolution towards redemption.

'The promise' is the promise given to Abraham which was fulfilled by the coming of Christ. This promise is put into operation by faith. Without the Law there would have been no sin, and without sin there would be no redemption.

'Faith in Jesus Christ', literally, 'faith *of* Jesus Christ', but see the notes on 2.16.

[23] This verse explains the thinking behind the previous verse. The main verb is repeated, **syngkleiomenoi**, 'being hemmed in', and Paul adds another verb, **ephrouroumetha**, 'we were being guarded'. The latter verb is used again by Paul in Phil. 4.7: 'And the peace of God which goes beyond all understanding will keep (**phrourêsei**) your hearts and minds in Christ Jesus.' Paul clearly sees God's purpose in imposing the Law as benevolent; he was protecting his people until such a time as they could be set free by Christ.

[24, 25] These verses echo the previous two verses and introduce a new image, that of the servant who takes the child to school, namely the **paidagôgos**, who stays with him all day acting as a bodyguard. It would be pressing the metaphor too far to take **eis Christon**, translated here as 'for Christ', i.e. until the time Christ should take over, as 'to Christ's (school)'.

26 For you are all children of God through your faith in Christ Jesus. 27 For all of you who have been baptized into Christ have put on Christ. 28 In him one is not Jew or Greek, one is not slave or freeman, one is not male or female, for you are all one in Christ Jesus. 29 If you are Christ's, then you are Abraham's seed, heirs according to the promise.

[26–29] This passage is really a summary of the whole of the chapter. Paul assures them that they are children of Abraham, that the promise given to Abraham applies to them, and that they are the true children of God because of their special relationship with Christ. Note the emphasis on 'all' in v. 26.

[26] 'Children', **huioi**, literally, 'sons'. The usual word for 'children' is **tekna**, but that word conveys a sense of immaturity. Paul has just said that they are no longer under a **paidagôgos**, that they are, in effect, adults. 'Sons' puts the emphasis on their legitimacy, their rights of inheritance and their close relationship with God the Father.

'Through your faith', **dia tês pisteôs**, i.e. the genitive case, not 'because of your faith', which would have been the meaning if the preposition **dia** had been followed by the accusative, i.e. **dia tên pistin**. It is a subtle but important distinction: their salvation comes not *because* they believe, as though themselves were the prime movers in the process of redemption, but *via* their belief, since Christ is the one who initiated the process and they are merely responding to him.

'In Christ Jesus', **en Christôi Iêsou**. There is an alternative reading, 'of Christ Jesus', but the meaning is the same.

[27] 'Have put on', **enedûsasthe**, has been treated by some commentators as a reference to the garments with which the newly baptized were clothed. This metaphor, however, is very common in contexts where there is no obvious reference to baptism. For example, we have putting on 'the armour of light' (Rom. 13.12), 'incorruption' and 'immortality' (I Cor. 15.53,54), 'the new man' (Eph. 4.24 and Col. 3.10), 'the full armour of God' (Eph. 6.11), 'the breastplate of righteousness' (Eph. 6.14), and 'the bowels of mercy, kindness, humility of thought, gentleness and patience' (Col. 3.12). The Septuagint also provides many examples of this metaphor.

[28] This verse is closely paralleled by Col. 3.11, 'where there is no Greek or Jew, circumcision or uncircumcision, barbarian, Scythian, slave or free, but [where] Christ is all and in all'. In

both passages we have the unusual word **eni** (an abbreviation of **enesti**), 'is included', 'is present', 'is possible', rather than the plain **esti**, 'is'. Lightfoot suggests translating **eni** as 'there is room for' or 'there is place for'. Paul is saying that, as far as their relationship with Christ goes, membership of the body of Christ is the same for all Christians; no one has a special relationship with him defined by nationality, gender or legal status. The NEB has 'There is no such thing as Jew and Greek . . .', but Paul is not saying that Greek and Jew do not exist, or that there is no difference between them considering other aspects of their relationship with each other. Other passages of Paul make it clear that he did recognize differences in social relationships, functions and behaviour between Jew and Greek, male and female, slave and free. In other words, there *was* such a thing as Jew and Greek.

It is very likely that this verse contains an allusion to a prayer familiar to every Jewish male, namely the thanksgiving, 'Blessed art thou, O Lord our God, King of the universe, who hast not made me a heathen. Blessed art thou . . . who hast not made me a bondman. Blessed art thou . . . who hast not made me a woman.' Paul is probably contrasting the exclusivity of Judaism with the inclusivity of Christianity.

[29] Because the Galatians are obsessed with the fear that they are not children of Abraham, Paul again makes the point that their relationship with Christ guarantees that they are true children of Abraham and heirs of his promise. The emphasis is made clear by the word order in Greek, the phrase 'heirs according to the promise (i.e. not according to the Law)' being placed at the end of the sentence.

Chapter 4

1 I tell you, as long as the heir is a child, he is no different from a slave, even if he is lord of everything, 2 but is under guardians and stewards until the day appointed by his father. 3 This is how it was with us – when we were children we were slaves under the elemental powers of the world. 4 But when the time of fulfilment came God sent out his son, born of a woman, born under the Law, 5 in order to redeem those under the Law, so that we might take up our adoption.

[1] 'Child', **nêpios**, literally, 'infant', Vulg. *parvulus*, but used here to denote 'a minor' of indeterminate age.

The term 'lord of everything' is not a reference to Christ but a hypothetical description of the child of the most powerful man in the world being potentially (i.e. as heir) himself 'lord of everything'. In other words, even if someone were the Emperor's son, he would still be equal to a slave until he reached the age of majority. Whether his father is alive or dead is irrelevant and we should not assume the father is already dead because the child is described as 'lord of everything'.

[2] 'Guardians', **epitropous**, i.e. legal representatives or trustees acting for the child; 'stewards', **oikonomous**, i.e.

managers of his property or household. When the term **epitropos** occurs elsewhere in the NT, Matt. 20.8 and Luke 8.3, both times it seems to denote 'steward'.

'Day appointed', **prothesmiâs**, a legal word denoting a fixed date by which certain actions, such as paying a sum of money or making a claim, would have to take place. The word is appropriate because Paul is using it as an allegory for the day predetermined by God for the redemption of mankind by the sacrifice of his son.

[3] 'The elemental powers of the world', **ta stoicheia tou kosmou**, Vulg. *elementis mundi*, are, according to a large number of the early Christian writers, the heavenly bodies which determine times and seasons, i.e. the sun, moon and stars. This usage is evidenced in II Peter 3.10,12, where the **stoicheia** are described as being destined to be consumed by flame at the end of the world. These elements can be described as enslaving the Jews because they determined the right days and times for rituals to take place, and the Gentiles were even more their slaves because they worshipped them as gods. It should be remembered that the important gods of Olympus such as Aphrodite, Hermes or Zeus were associated with the planets and each had a particular day of the week devoted to them. A passage from Colossians (2.20–21) is so relevant that it should be quoted in full: 'If you have escaped by death with Christ *from the elemental powers of the world* (**apo tôn stoicheiôn tou kosmou**), why do you subject yourselves as though you are living in the world to ordinances, such as, "don't handle, don't taste, don't touch"?' This passage clearly seems to connect the dietary laws and purificatory regulations of Judaism with enslavement to the **stoicheia tou kosmou**.

On the other hand, a small number of early scholars interpreted the phrase as 'elementary teaching', i.e. an elementary stage in human theological education which has now been superseded by a more mature knowledge of God. The phrase was thus taken as analogous with **hê sophiâ tou kosmou**, 'the wisdom of the world', found in I Cor. 1.20 and 3.19. **Ta stoicheia** frequently means 'the letters of the alphabet', and so can be extended to mean 'elementary knowledge', as in Heb. 5.12, where we find '**ta stoicheia** of the beginning of the sayings of God', which I translate as 'the basic principles of God's word'.

The major objection to the latter interpretation being appropriate here is that it is difficult to see how such an interpretation can apply to the Gentiles' former understanding of God. It certainly would apply to Paul's view of the elementary teaching embodied in the Jewish Law and would describe the former state of Jewish Christians, but it is patently absurd to believe that the Gentiles had once observed this Law. Verse 9 refers to the Galatians wanting to *return* to the 'feeble, inadequate **stoicheia** and to be their slaves all over again'. This would imply that the Galatian Gentiles had once observed the Jewish Law, although the whole subject of this letter is their desire to adopt the Law *for the first time* by undergoing circumcision. Whatever interpretation we accept, it must cover both Jews and Gentiles. Some commentators treat the references to 'us' and 'we' in vv. 3 and 5 as referring only to Jews, but vv. 8 and 9 make it clear that the enslavement to **ta stoicheia** applied to Gentiles as well.

[4] 'Time of fulfilment', **plêrôma tou chronou**, literally, 'fullness of time'.

'Born of a woman, born under the Law', i.e. a Jew. We tend to think that the point Paul is making is that God's son became a man. In fact, he is making a different point altogether: God's son became a Jew. Jesus was a Jew because his mother was Jewish. Jewish law has always defined a Jew as one born of a Jewish mother. One of the crucial issues facing Judaism today is the question of Jewish identity. Since Reform Judaism in America in 1983 decided to treat as Jewish the child of a Jewish

father and a non-Jewish mother, subject to certain conditions
being met, there is a danger of a major schism in Judaism that,
according to J. Sacks (*Faith in the Future*, p. 235), 'will parallel
the Jewish-Christian schism nineteen centuries ago'.

Why is Paul stressing the Jewishness of Christ? Because
Christ by virtue of being a Jew was subject to the Law. The
redemption of mankind depended on this.

[5] 'Redeem', **exagorasêi,** literally, 'buy up' or 'buy off'. The
same verb is used in 3.13.

'Take up our adoption', **tên huiothesiân apolabômen.**
Huiothesiâ is 'adoption as sons' not 'sonship'. Christ is the true
son of God; we are adopted sons and daughters. The verb
apolabômen can mean 'regain' or 'recover', which would
imply that we were once sons of God but lost our sonship, as
Augustine believed, due to Adam's fall. The Vulgate translates
this verb as *reciperemus,* i.e. 'regain', which supports
Augustine's interpretation, but the Greek original can mean
'receive' as well as 'regain'.

'We' refers to all Christians, Jewish and Gentile, because true
sonship comes through the promise given to Abraham, as has
been made clear in the previous chapter, and not through
observation of the Mosaic Law. The process of redemption,
however, starts with those under the Law, i.e. the Jews, and
then is extended to the Gentiles, as Peter says to his Jewish
audience (Acts 3.26), 'To you first . . .' Because Christ was
born a Jew his gospel was preached first to Jews, although
non-Jews were clearly involved as well, and after the resurrec-
tion his apostles preached the gospel first to Jews and only later
to Gentiles.

6 And because you are sons, God has sent out into our
hearts his son's spirit which cries out 'Abba (that is,
Father)!' 7 So you are no longer a slave but a son, and if

a son, then you are also an heir through God. 8 But at that time when you did not know God, you were slaves of those who are essentially not gods. 9 Now, however, knowing God, or rather being known by him, how can you turn back again to those feeble, inadequate elements and want to be their slaves all over again? 10 You observe days, months, seasons and years – 11 I am afraid for you in case I have sweated over you for nothing.

[6] 'Our', **hêmôn**, is surprising after 'because *you* are sons', but this shift in person is not uncommon with Paul. There is an alternative reading, **hûmôn**, 'your', but it is not found in the best manuscripts, and we should resist the temptation to tidy up the grammar. In later Greek the two words would have the same pronunciation, but that is still no excuse for adopting the reading **hûmôn**. Paul identifies himself so closely with his audience that the shift in person is understandable. It is not unreasonable to interpret this and other grammatical peculiarities as a sign of emotional involvement.

'His son's spirit' is probably another way of referring to the Holy Spirit, though we need not insist on this.

[7] As another instance of the grammatical peculiarity which we found in the previous verse, we now have the person 'you' (singular) where we might have expected the plural.

'An heir through God' is the best reading. There are other readings, such as 'an heir of God, and a joint heir with Christ' and 'an heir of God through Christ', variations which would indicate that Paul's expression was not easily understood. It is, however, typical of Paul's condensed style. He is making the point that we are heirs of the kingdom not through our own merit but by the action of God.

[8] The reference to not knowing God (**ouk eidotes Theon**) must mean that Paul is addressing a Gentile audience. See the notes on v. 3. They are described as slaves, but their slavery was obviously not subjection to the Law or some elementary theological doctrine. 'Those who are essentially not gods', **tois physei mê ousin theois**, literally, 'those by nature not being gods', are the **stoicheia** of vv. 3 and 9.

[9] There are several verbs for 'know' in Greek, and here Paul uses **gnontes**, from **ginôskô**, to express knowledge of a person, recognition or learning by observation. The verb he uses in the previous verse, **eidotes**, from **oida**, is the more general word used to denote having knowledge of some fact or knowing how to do something. Paul amends his statement about knowing God because it is impossible for human beings really to know God in the sense in which he knows us, and because God makes the first move in the process of reconciliation which allows us to get to know him.

'Feeble, inadequate', **asthenê kai ptôcha**, literally, 'weak and beggarly', i.e. they have no power and are too poor to give any real benefits. God, by contrast, is both strong and bountiful.

[10] The reference to observing 'days, months, seasons and years' indicates that the Galatians were not only interested in being circumcised but were already keeping the major Jewish festivals and holy days, presumably sabbaths, new moons, and annual festivals such as the Passover and Tabernacles. The reference to 'years' presumably covers jubilees and ceremonies such as the *bar mitzvah*.

[11] This verse, the next one and the previous one, which has been interrupted, have no connecting particles (words like 'for', 'but', 'however', etc.) such as we normally find in Greek prose, and this is probably indicative of the emotion and stress

Paul is feeling. 'I have sweated', literally, 'I have tired myself out', or 'I have toiled', **kekopiâka**, is a strong expression.

12 Be as I am, brethren, because I am as you are, I beseech you. You did me no wrong. 13 Indeed you know when I preached the gospel to you the first time due to my sickness, 14 although my physical state was a trial to you, you did not scorn or reject me, but received me as [though I was] an angel of God, as [if I was] Christ Jesus. 15 Where then [is] the blessing you gave me? For I bear witness for you that if [it had been] possible you would have dug out your eyes and given them to me. 16 So have I become your enemy by telling you the truth?

[12] This verse is not easy because verbs have been omitted. The literal meaning of the first part is 'Become as I, because I also as you'. Some commentators suggest that the missing verb in the second clause is 'was' and translate it, 'Become as I *am*, because I *was* also like you'. This presumably means that Paul was also in bondage like them to the elemental powers but has now freed himself and is asking them to be like he is now. The better suggestion is that the missing verb is 'became', and thus we would read, 'Become as I *have become*, because I *became* like you.' Paul is saying, in other words, that he became a Gentile and abandoned the old Law when he preached the gospel to the Galatians. All he asks is that they should be Gentile Christians, not Jewish ones.

'You did me no wrong': a sudden change of subject. Paul now reminds them how well he was treated by them in the early days. He continues this theme in the next three verses. Some detect in this sentence a sub-text, 'you never disobeyed me in the past, so don't disobey me now', but this is reading too much into the statement.

[13] It is clear that the 'sickness', **astheneian tês sarkos**, literally, 'weakness of the flesh', was the actual reason why Paul preached to the Galatians. We have to presume that he could not travel because he was too ill and was detained in the area. Some commentators have attempted to translate the phrase **di'astheneian** as though it means 'through', i.e. 'during my illness', but this is not grammatically possible.

The real problem occurs when we try to find out what this **astheneia** was. The Vulgate translates the phrase as *per infirmitatem carnis* and gives an ambiguity to the phrase which the Greek does not have. Hence some have imagined a reference to some carnal or spiritual temptation of the Galatians: 'due to the weakness of *your* flesh', or even Paul's 'weakness of the flesh' in giving in to the Judaizers and circumcising Timothy, or some other spiritual trials. Passing on to the more plausible suggestions, we find that the most popular one amongst early commentators was that Paul was laid low by some form of severe headache or migraine. Ophthalmia has also been suggested due to the statement that the Galatians were willing to give Paul their own eyes. In the absence of firm evidence we can only make one more suggestion, namely, that Paul was recovering from the effects of the stoning mentioned in Acts 14.19.

[14] 'Although my physical state was a trial to you, you did not scorn or reject me', literally, '*you did* not scorn or *reject*, **exeptysate** (literally, 'spit out'), *the trial of you*, **ton peirasmon hûmôn**, in my flesh.' As Lightfoot says, this refers to Paul's 'bodily ailment which was a trial to the Galatians and which might have led them to reject his preaching'. As usual the problem is caused by Paul's condensed style of expression. It caused problems to early interpreters too, because we have an alternative reading in some of the manuscripts which, instead of **hûmôn**, 'of you', gives **mou**, 'of me' or 'my'. This is the reading followed by the AV, which translates this passage as

follows: 'and *my* temptation which was in my flesh ye despised not, nor rejected'.

'Angel' or 'messenger', **angelon**.

[15] 'The blessing you gave', literally, 'your blessing', **ho makarismos hûmôn,** has been frequently mistranslated, probably due to a misunderstanding of the Vulg. *beatitudo vestra.* Tyndale, for instance, translates, 'How happy were ye then', and the A V, 'Where is then the blessedness ye spake of?' It is not, however, the blessing that Paul conferred on them but their blessing of him that is referred to here. He is comparing the pleasant things they said about him at their first meeting with the unpleasant things they are saying about him now.

Again we have variant readings in inferior manuscripts which include the addition of **ên,** 'was', to supply the missing verb.

[16] This verse contrasts their present hostility with their previous friendliness.

17 They are running after you for no good reason. They want to exclude you so that you should run after them. 18 It is good to show enthusiasm in a good cause at all times and not only when I am with you. 19 My babies, I am suffering labour pains again over you until Christ is formed in you. 20 I wanted to be with you just now and to try another way of talking because I am at a loss what to do with you.

[17] Paul is talking about the motives of the Judaizers who are putting pressure on the Galatians. There is a word-play in vv. 17 and 18 which cannot be easily translated. 'They are running after', **zêlousin,** literally, 'strive for', from the same root from which we derive 'zealot' a word which has special significance

in the context of the Jewish War which broke out in AD 66. The name 'Zealot', i.e. 'Enthusiast', was the title chosen by a group of intolerant bigots (the sort of group which we might find today in the Middle East described as militant fundamentalists). These Zealots attempted to eliminate the more moderate parties in Judaea. In v.18 the word is picked up again in the form **zêlousthai**, 'to show enthusiasm'.

'Exclude', **ekkleisai**, from **ekkleiô**, 'I shut out' (nothing to do with **ekklêsiâ**, which is derived from **ekkaleô**, 'I call out'), i.e. from the privileges of being a Jew. In other words, they are creating a situation where the Galatians are being tempted to join an exclusive club, entry to which is granted on circumcision. The technique is familiar in marketing circles. If you want to sell anything, advertise it as expensive and only available to a few chosen and discriminating people.

[18] There seems to be a sudden shift of thought in this verse. Paul starts by saying that enthusiasm is sometimes a good thing, commenting, presumably, on the enthusiasm of the Judaizers, then he recommends enthusiasm to the Galatians, and adds that they should be enthusiastic even when he is not with them. As usual, his mind is too fast for his words. If we were to expand this verse to express his chain of thought it would run, 'There is nothing wrong with showing zeal in a good cause, although those people are being zealous in a bad cause. You should be enthusiastic in a good cause and all the time. By the way, you seem to lack enthusiasm when it is needed for a good cause and have plenty of enthusiasm for some bad cause when I am not with you.'

The Vulgate translates the first part of this verse *bonum aemulamini*, 'strive after the good', because it is based on a text which had **zêlousthe** (imperative: 'strive') instead of **zêlousthai** (passive infinitive: 'to be striven after'). This corruption of the text is due to the fact that the diphthong **ai** was already starting to sound like the short vowel **e**, as in modern Greek.

[19] The pain felt by Paul when writing this and the next verse is almost tangible. Firstly he uses **teknia**, 'little children', a diminutive common ·in John but not found elsewhere in the NT. Scholars, aware that the word is not used by Paul outside this passage, have emended it to the more usual **tekna**, 'children', a reading found even in some good manuscripts. The fact, however, that Paul does not use **teknia** elsewhere is not a good reason to emend, since he rarely uses **tekna** either in the vocative case as it is used here. The Vulgate is based on the reading **teknia** which it translates as *filioli* (the corresponding diminutive in Latin). It is simplistic to reject a reading, or to doubt the authorship of a passage, purely on the grounds that the author does not use the word elsewhere.

Secondly, this is the only place in Paul where the verb **ôdînô**, 'I am in travail', is found, apart from its occurrence in v. 27 of this chapter, where it is used non-metaphorically in a quotation from the Septuagint. It only occurs once in the rest of the NT, in Rev. 12.2, but again it is not used metaphorically in that passage. Incidentally, the noun **ôdîn** (plural **ôdînes**), 'birth pain[s]', is found four times in the NT. Paul, of course, is using the verb as a vivid metaphor of childbirth. The pain of the process is uppermost in his thought rather than the actual process of giving birth because he proceeds to use another unique metaphor, 'until Christ is formed in you'. Attempts to link the process of giving birth with the supposed forming of the embryo into a child are not very believable and we should not try to see consistency where none is intended. The metaphor of forming, **morphôsis**, is more appropriate when applied to the growth of the child into the perfect, mature adult.

[20] 'Try another way of talking', **allaxai tên phônên mou**, literally, 'alter my voice'. Paul, however, is referring not to changing his tone of voice but to changing his approach. His frustration is very real and we need not treat his statement that he was at a loss as a mere rhetorical exaggeration.

21 Tell me, you who want to be under the Law, don't you hear the Law? 22 For it is written that Abraham had two sons, one by the slave girl and the other by the free woman. 23 But the child of the slave girl was born according to the flesh, while the child of the free woman was born through the promise. 24 This is an allegory; these women are the two covenants, one [is] from Mount Sinai who gives birth into slavery and she is Hagar. 25 The Mount Sinai of Hagar is in Arabia, and corresponds with Jerusalem today, for she is a slave along with her children. 26 But the Jerusalem above is free and she is our mother.

[21] Like a rabbi who has suddenly found a *hiddush*, that is, a new meaning in scripture that no one has spotted before, Paul finds in the Law, i.e. the *Torah* as Scripture, another argument to persuade those who will only be persuaded by evidence from the Law.

'Don't you hear?', **ouk akouete**, seemed such an odd way of appealing to scripture that the text was altered in some manuscripts to read **ouk anaginôskete**, 'Don't you read?' It is, however, an echo of the authentic voice of the rabbi who would ask, 'What does the *Torah* say?' Paul is in effect saying, 'Hear the Law' with emphasis, i.e. 'Surely you hear the Law?'

[22] The story of the children of Sarah and Hagar is told in Genesis 16–21.

[23] 'According to the flesh', **kata sarka**, is not simply a reference to a carnal relationship with a woman who is not Abraham's official wife, but is rather to be taken as the opposite of **kata pneuma**, 'according to the spirit'. Without going into Paul's doctrine of **sarx** and **pneuma**, which he has

explained in more detail in Romans, and which we shall look at briefly in reference to 5.17, it may be said that the significance here is that Ishmael was born, as Lightfoot puts it, 'in the common course of nature', while Isaac was born as a result of God's miraculous intervention when Sarah was past child-bearing age. The birth of Isaac was part of the promise and the covenant offered to Abraham. As we have already seen, the promise given to Abraham forms the basis for the redemption of all human beings through faith in Christ.

[24] The women Hagar and Sarah stand for the two cov-enants. Hagar represents the Mosaic Law which was delivered from Mount Sinai, whereas Sarah represents the new covenant of Christ which comes directly from the heavenly Jerusalem.

The use of the term 'allegory' does not imply that Paul did not accept the story as historically true. He uses the term as a synonym for 'type', **typos**. In other words, he sees a deeper significance in a story which has its own factual validity.

[25] Chrysostom argued that the name of Mount Sinai was the same as Hagar in the language spoken in the neighbourhood of Sinai, but Paul is not using such an argument here. It is true that there is an Arabic word for 'rock' or 'stone' similar to the name Hagar, but we need not develop the theme. Paul equates Hagar with the Mosaic Law, and Sinai with the earthly Jerusalem. A similar allegory is found in Heb. 12.18–24, where the terror associated with the earthly Mount Sinai, representing the Mosaic Law, is contrasted with the joy of the heavenly Jerusalem, which stands for the new covenant of Christ. Paul also sees a connection between the slavery of Hagar and the slavery of the Jews under the Law, so at the same time he is equating Hagar with the Jews. The matter is not made easier by the fact that there are several variations of the text in this verse.

[26] Paul omits to mention that Sarah was equated with the

new covenant. In v. 24 Hagar represents one of the two covenants, but Paul does not complete the equation for the other woman. He now seems to equate Sarah with the new Jerusalem, as well as with the new covenant, because it is described as free and our mother. It is significant that Paul uses a name for Jerusalem closer to the Hebrew than the normal Greek name for the city, i.e. **Hierousalêm** and not **Hierosolyma**. The first is sacred and theological, while the second is factual and geographical. One might say that the first is **kata pneuma** while the second is **kata sarka**.

Sarah is very important in rabbinical tradition. We have already noted the significance of her name in the note on 3.6. There is a touching account (D. Goldstein, *Jewish Legends*, pp. 53–4) of her having so much milk in her breasts when Isaac was born that she was able to feed all the local infants. The story goes on to say that these children grew up to be the ancestors of sincere converts to Judaism and the righteous Gentiles.

27 For it is written, 'Rejoice you barren one, you who do not give birth, break loose and shout, you who do not labour in travail, because the children of the one left desolate are more numerous than those of the one with a man.' 28 And you, my brothers and sisters, are children of the promise following Isaac. 29 But as at that time the one born according to the flesh persecuted the one born according to the spirit, so it is now. 30 But what does the scripture say? 'Expel the slave girl and her son; for the son of the slave girl shall not be an heir along with the son of the free woman.' 31 Therefore, brothers and sisters, we are not children of a slave girl but the free woman.

[27] This quotation from the Sept. version of Isa. 54.1 is intended by Paul to be applicable to Sarah, who gave birth to Isaac when she was past child-bearing age. The parallel cannot be pressed too far, since Sarah had a husband. It is interesting to note that the passage from Isaiah goes on to say in v. 5 (AV), 'For thy Maker is thy husband; the Lord of hosts is his name; and thy Redeemer the Holy One of Israel; the God of the whole earth shall he be called.' This messianic passage fits in with Paul's suggestion above in v. 26 that Sarah is a type of the new Jerusalem.

There is an interesting exposition of this passage in an early letter attributed on poor evidence to Clement of Rome, which is supposed to have been sent to the Corinthians (II Clem. 2.1–3): 'When he said, "Rejoice you barren one, you who do not give birth," he meant us. For our church was barren before she was given children. And when he said, "Shout, you who do not labour in travail," he means the following: we should offer up our prayers to God in simplicity, and not be remiss like women in labour. And when he said, "Because the children of the one left desolate are more numerous than those of the one with a man," it was because our people seemed to be abandoned by God, but now we who have believed have become more numerous than those who think they have God.'

Leaving aside the singularly implausible reference to the neglect of prayer on the part of women in labour, we can see that the passage from Isaiah continued to be used in the early church as material for arguing the superiority of Christianity to Judaism.

[28] This is a summary of the secondary argument which traces the continuing application of the promise given to Abraham and passed on through Sarah's son Isaac and his descendants.

'You', **hûmeis,** is probably a better reading than the alternative **hêmeis,** 'we', found in some good manuscripts.

[29] 'The one born according to the flesh', i.e. Ishmael.

'Persecuted', **ediôken**, seems rather a strong expression for Ishmael's mocking of Sarah on the occasion of the feast Abraham gave to celebrate the weaning of Isaac (Gen. 21.9), but Paul is trying to find a parallel with the Jewish opposition to Christianity in the account of Ishmael's bad behaviour. The relations between the two brothers were regarded as significant in rabbinical tradition, especially in reference to the Arabs, and later the Muslims, who were identified with Ishmael's descendants.

[30] The quotation comes from Gen. 21.10 and records Sarah's angry reaction to Ishmael's mocking. There are slight variations from the Sept. version from which this quotation comes; Paul, for instance, substitutes 'with the son of the free woman' for the Sept. 'with my son Isaac'.

[31] In this verse Paul repeats the theme of vv. 26 and 28, using slightly different wording, probably because the opposition were insisting on the contrary, i.e. that the Gentile Christians were not true children of Sarah but of Hagar.

Chapter 5

1 Christ freed us for freedom; so stand firm [in it] and do not be subject again to the yoke of slavery. 2 Look, I, Paul, am telling you that if you are circumcised, Christ will be no advantage to you. 3 I declare again to every man who is being circumcised that he is a debtor to perform the whole of the Law. 4 You who are justified by the Law have been severed from Christ, you have been banished from grace.

[1] Some commentators have joined the first part of this verse with the last verse of the previous chapter using a relative pronoun found in some manuscripts and producing a sentence with the meaning, 'we are not children of a slave girl but the free woman, by [virtue of] the freedom *with which* (**hêi**) Christ has freed us. So stand firm and . . ., etc.' Alternatively, they translate, 'we are not children of a slave girl but *of the woman who is free* with the freedom . . ., etc.' Both suggestions lack plausibility and depend on a dubious reading. The text makes perfect sense as it stands. 'Christ freed us for freedom' is a condensed way of saying, 'Christ freed us in order that we should be free', a concept repeated in v. 13 of this chapter, 'for you were called to freedom'. Admittedly the phrase 'to freedom', **ep'eleutheriâi**, in v.13 contains the preposition **epi**, 'for' or 'to', and in this verse we have **eleutheriâi** with no preposition but preceded by the definite article **têi**. The fact that

there is no preposition nor, for that matter, any connecting particle is not important. The dative here is probably best regarded as a variety of relative dative, i.e. 'with regard to', hence 'for the purpose of'. Paul's use or non-use of the preposition **en** with the dative is also inconsistent, as we see in v. 4 (**en nomôi**, 'by the Law') and in v. 5 (**pneumati**, 'by/in the spirit'), and when he is under stress he frequently neglects to insert a particle, as I have mentioned in the notes on 4.11. Incidentally, some readers might be confused by references to a case which can be translated by so many prepositions, especially those who know Latin and are familiar with the distinction between the dative and the ablative cases of that language. One should note that in Greek the case we call the dative (to, for) also acts as an instrumental (by, with).

'Be subject', **enechesthe**, from **enechomai**, a legal term, 'be bound by' or 'be liable to'. **Enechomai** is found nowhere else in the NT.

[2] The vehemence of Paul's opposition to the suggestion that the Galatians should be circumcised is clear from the colloquial and personal tone of this verse. 'Look here, it's me, yes, Paul, talking!' Compare the more gentle but still insistent tone of the beginning of II Cor. 10.1, 'I myself, I, Paul, beseech you . . .'.

[3] 'I declare' (or 'I protest'), **martûromai**, a verb used when one makes a solemn declaration in the presence of witnesses, and in a pagan context frequently in the presence of the gods whom one calls to witness. The much commoner verb **martyreô**, 'I bear witness' or 'I testify', does not carry the same strength of meaning.

'Being circumcised', i.e. contemplating circumcision, is applied, not as one would expect, to the male word for 'man', i.e. **anêr**, but to the generic term for 'man', i.e. 'human being', **anthrôpos**. In effect, Paul is warning both men and women not to be subject to the Law's regulations. Although obviously circumcision only applies physically to men, Paul knows that for both sexes it is the most potent symbol of Jewish religious practices.

'Debtor to perform' is another way of saying 'is obliged to perform'.

[4] 'Are justified by the Law', or rather 'are attempting to be justified by the Law'.

'Severed', **katêrgêthête,** from the verb **katargeô,** which is a word Paul is fond of using, most frequently in the sense of 'make redundant', 'abolish', 'annul'. It is used only three times in the NT with the preposition **apo,** 'from', twice in the sense of 'free', 'deliver', and here in the sense of 'separate', 'cut off'.

'You have been banished' translates the idiomatic **exepesate,** which literally means 'you have fallen out (from)'. **Ekballô,** 'I banish', literally, 'I throw out', often uses as its passive the verb **ekpiptô,** 'I fall out'.

5 For we await the hope of righteousness in the spirit from faith. 6 For in Christ Jesus neither circumcision nor uncircumcision has any power but faith operating through love [does]. 7 You were making good progress; who thwarted your obedience to the truth? 8 This persuading [does] not [come] from him who calls you. 9 A little yeast makes all the dough rise.

[5] 'Hope of righteousness' refers to a future state of righteousness. In other words the state of righteousness, of having been made just, is a continuous process which is only completed when the course has been run. See the notes on 2.16 *re* 'justification'.

'In the spirit', **pneumati,** could mean 'in one's spirit', 'spiritually', or 'in/by the Holy Spirit'. Even if Paul had used the preposition **en,** it would not be clear whether we should translate **pneumati** as 'in the spirit' or 'by the spirit'. Incidentally, there is no definite article before any noun in this verse, although grammatically we might expect it to be used before 'spirit', 'faith', 'hope' and 'righteousness'. As I have already pointed out in the notes on 2.16, Paul shows no consistent pattern in his use of the definite article.

[6] 'Faith operating through love', **pistis di'agapês energoumenê**, is faith that is manifested by acts of love. 'Love', **agapê**, is not a warm feeling but a spiritual state defining and defined by an active relationship with God and other individuals. This verse clearly contradicts the notion that Paul is attacking works or that he visualizes them as diametrically opposed to faith.

(*A note for those who know some Greek*) **Energoumenê** is a middle, not a passive participle. In other words, here it does not mean 'being worked upon'. The middle voice of the verb **energeô** is often used in the NT in reference to abstract forces working on the personality, e.g. the word of God, emotions, death, hidden lawlessness, etc. The active is mostly, but not always, used to refer to God himself working. For example, in 2.8, '**energêsâs** (having worked) through Peter in the mission of circumcision, also **enêrgêsen** (worked) through me in regard to the Gentiles', and in 3.5, '**energôn** (working) acts of power in you'.

[7] 'You were making good progress', **etrechete kalôs**, literally, 'you were running well'.

'Thwarted', **enekopsen**, literally, 'knocked in', a term used in a military context to denote breaking up roads or bridges. The opposite is **prokoptô**, 'clear the way', 'act as a pioneer', used in 1.14 in the sense 'outstrip'.

[8] 'Persuading', **peismonê**, is probably the act of persuading

rather than the state of being persuaded. This is the only place it is found in the NT.

[9] This metaphor is used in I Cor. 5.6 in reference to the unwelcome presence of a member of the church who had married his father's wife. We tend to think of yeast as a good thing and therefore might use the metaphor approvingly to describe a person who takes a lead in introducing some positive development. If we wish to comment unfavourably, our negative metaphor is the bad apple. Here and in I Corinthians Paul is thinking of people whose actions are regarded as negative. Why is yeast regarded as unwelcome? Probably because the metaphor derives from the Passover preparations when the Jewish housewife clears out every scrap of yeast from her kitchen before making the unleavened bread and other Passover dishes.

10 I have confidence in you through the Lord that you will not change your minds; and the one causing you this trouble will be judged, whoever he is. 11 As for me, brethren, if I am still proclaiming circumcision, why am I still being persecuted? So then, the stumbling block of the cross has been removed. 12 I wish those unsettling you would cut themselves off. 13 For you were called to freedom, brethren; only do not [use] your freedom as an opportunity for the flesh but serve one another with love.

[10] 'Through the Lord', **en kûriôi**, literally, 'in [the] Lord'. Note the absence of the definite article.

'Change your minds', i.e. adopt Jewish practices such as circumcision.

'Be judged', **bastasei to krima,** literally, 'bear the condemnation'.

[11] This verse requires some explanation. In the first place, the reference to Paul proclaiming circumcision is to be understood as a charge levelled at him by those who used his circumcision of Timothy (Acts 16.3) as evidence that Paul approved the universal application of the practice. Paul points out that he would not be attacked by the Judaizers if he approved of circumcision. He then goes on to say ironically, 'Since I obviously am in favour of circumcision and of returning to observance of the Law, I can get rid of the need to make our faith depend on the crucifixion of Christ. So now the great stumbling block is removed.'

'The stumbling block of the cross', **to skandalon tou staurou**, is the doctrine of the atonement by the sacrifice of the Messiah, as Paul says in I Cor. 1.23, 'We proclaim Christ crucified, a stumbling block to the Jews and foolishness to the Gentiles.' It is not just the curse and shame of crucifixion which prevented the Jews from accepting Christ as their saviour but the fact that the Messiah should have been put to death instead of leading their nation to victory over their enemies. To accept the crucified Christ was to reject the Law and all that they believed in. The stumbling block is the hurdle of faith the Jew and the Gentile alike have to jump if they want to become Christians.

[12] Paul suddenly turns on his enemies with an expression so violent that one is tempted to take it metaphorically. He wishes that those who want to mutilate the Galatians would mutilate themselves. 'Cut off', **apokopsontai**, refers to castration. The verb **apokoptô** is used to refer to cutting off hands or feet in Mark 9.43, 45 and to cutting off ears in John 18.10, 26. The verb is not used metaphorically in the NT, and the middle form **apokoptomai** used here frequently refers to self-castration. Lightfoot points out that Pessinus, one of the major cities in Galatia, was the home of the cult of the goddess Cybele, whose priests castrated themselves in a frenzied public ceremony. It is, however, possible that Paul is saying, 'I wish those wanting to

cut bits off you would cut themselves off from the body of the church', but it seems more likely that this is a heavy joke against his opponents and is meant to raise a laugh, not a shudder.

[13] 'As an opportunity' or 'as a pretext', **eis aphormên**, literally, 'as a base of operations'. Paul turns to those in his audience who are not tempted to Judaize and warns them not to regard the freedom that Christ has given them as a reason for selfish indulgence or living in an immoral way. The word 'only', **monon**, is to be taken as qualifying his assertion of their liberty. The danger of abandoning the Law, **nomos**, is that they might be tempted to abandon all moral laws, i.e. become antinomians.

'With love', **dia tês agapês**, literally, 'through love'. That is, service to their fellow members is the expression of love. They are not to use their freedom for self-gratification. A few manuscripts have an alternative reading for this phrase, 'with the love of the spirit', **têi agapêi tou pneumatos**. This looks like a gloss which has ousted the original reading that it was intended to explain.

14 For the fulfilment of the whole Law is expressed in one statement – 'you shall love your neighbour as yourself'. 15 But if you bite or devour one another, watch out lest you be destroyed by one another. 16 I say to you, walk in the spirit and do not indulge the desire of the flesh. 17 For the desire of the flesh is against the spirit, and the spirit's desire is against the flesh, for these are opposed to one another, so that you may not do whatever you want to do. 18 If you are driven by the spirit, you are not under the Law.

[14] The quotation is from Lev. 19.18 and occurs elsewhere in

the NT. The most famous occurrence is in the account of Jesus' reply to the 'lawyer', i.e. the student of the Law (see Matt. 22.34–40, Mark 12.28–34 and Luke 10.25–28). Matthew and Mark make it clear that the most important, i.e. the first, commandment was the one which refers to loving God. Loving one's neighbour is the second commandment. Luke, incidentally, does not use the terms 'first' or 'second'.

The literal translation of the opening of this verse is, 'For the whole Law has been fulfilled in one saying, that is, etc.' The verb **peplêrôtai** does not mean 'is summed up' but 'is fulfilled'. Paul is saying that *the fulfilment* of the Law can be summed up by one commandment, not that the Law can be summed up by one commandment. He is answering the question 'How can I fulfil the Law?', not the question 'How would you sum up the Law?'

[15] 'Bite', **daknete**, and 'devour', **katesthiete**, are metaphors derived from the behaviour of wild animals.

[16] 'Walk in the spirit', **pneumati peripateite**, i.e. live a life guided by the Holy Spirit.

'Indulge', i.e. 'grant the fulfilment of', is more appropriate here than 'fulfil' as a translation of **telesête**. The verb is often found in the sense of 'glut'.

[17] Paul's doctrine of 'flesh' and 'spirit' is not easy to explain briefly. It is, however, important to note that Paul does not think of the human body as sinful or regard matter as evil and spirit as good. He did not subscribe to the Gnostic or Platonist view of the material world as intrinsically evil. 'Flesh' in Paul's writings stands for the essential nature of human beings as distinct from the nature of God. 'Flesh' includes man's thoughts and desires, and it represents his weakness and frailty. 'Flesh' is morally neither good nor bad, but it provides the environment where sin can take hold and flourish. Christ

became flesh but did not become sinful. This is a complicated picture, since Paul's concept of the battle between 'flesh' and 'spirit' is close to the rabbinical notion of the battle between the good and the evil impulses which fight for domination in the human soul. 'Flesh' is potentially evil because it can be corrupted, and when it opposes 'spirit' it is allowing sin a foothold. We should not, incidentally, think of the sins of the flesh as just sexual sins. Pride and anger are as much sins of the flesh as fornication is.

'Whatever you want to do' includes things you should not do. There is nothing wrong in doing what you want to do provided what you want to do is right. Paul is commenting on the sinfulness of giving in to every desire.

[18] If one allows the spirit to take over the running of one's life, one does not need to be subject to the Law.

'You are driven', **agesthe**, rather than 'you are led', is a more dynamic concept of the force of the spirit.

19 The works of the flesh are obvious; they are fornication, impurity, hooliganism, 20 idolatry, witchcraft, hostility, strife, rivalry, anger, intrigues, dissensions, sectarianism, 21 envy, drunkenness, revelry, and such like, and I tell you, as I have told you before, that those who do such things shall not inherit the kingdom of God.

[19] The previous verse would cause his audience to ask how one can know one is actually being led by the spirit. Paul gives a list of the activities that would indicate one is *not* being led by the spirit. Some manuscripts add a fourth vice, i.e. **moicheiâ**, 'adultery', to the list but there is no warrant for this since Paul puts the same three vices together in II Cor. 12.21.

'Impurity', **akatharsiâ**, is any immoral sexual activity not covered by 'fornication', **porneiâ**. There is no evidence for translating **akatharsiâ** as 'covetousness'. In I Thess. 2.3 it seems to denote either the supposed impurity of Paul in abandoning the Law and consorting with Gentiles, or a perverted interest in peddling libertine notions.

'Hooliganism', **aselgeia**, rather than 'wantonness', 'sensuality', although the latter meanings are found. **Aselgeia** denotes any outrageous behaviour, particularly wanton violence. It does not necessarily carry any sexual overtone.

[20] 'Witchcraft', **pharmakeiâ**, covers a wide range of sins from casting spells to using magic potions. The basic meaning is the use of drugs for immoral purposes.

'Hostility, strife, rivalry', **echthrai, eris, zêlos**, represent an ascending scale ranging from general uncharitable feelings, through actual quarrels to the pursuing of one's own interests in a hostile manner. 'Anger', **thûmoi**, in the plural, i.e. 'outbursts of passion', takes one further up the scale. 'Intrigues', **erîtheiai**, originally denoting canvassing, hence intriguing, for a public office, represent the next stage, where negative emotions have culminated in deliberate and calculated sinful activities. Selfish ambition in pursuing money or status is probably the meaning intended here. Incidentally, in II Cor. 12.20 we have the identical list, 'strife, rivalry, anger, intrigues', which would suggest that it was a part of Paul's standard teaching on morality.

'Dissensions', **dichostasiai**, literally, 'standing[s] apart', and 'sectarianism', **haireseis**, i.e. 'factions' (not 'heresies'), represent the result of hostile behaviour.

[21] Several manuscripts add **phonoi**, 'murders', after **phthonoi**, 'envy', probably because the two words occur together in Rom. 1.29.

'Revelry', **kômoi**, means rather more than 'going to parties' or 'merry-making'. The original application of this word is to the drunken procession of worshippers in some pagan ceremony. The association of **kômoi** with drunkenness is also found in Rom. 13.13. In I Peter 4.3 we have 'wine-swilling, revelry (**kômois**), drinking and lawless idolatries'.

'The kingdom of God' here is God's heavenly kingdom and is a future inheritance. The use of the future tense of 'inherit' with 'the kingdom of God' is paralleled in I Cor. 6.9,10, where again we have a list of the sins which earn disqualification.

22 But the fruit of the spirit is love, joy, peace, patience, kindness, goodness, faith, 23 gentleness and self-control; against such there is no Law. 24 Those who [are] of Christ have crucified the flesh together with its troubles and desires. 25 If we live by the spirit, let us also walk by the spirit. 26 Let us not be conceited, provoking one another, bearing grudges against one another.

[22] In contrast to the 'works of the flesh', which indicate that one is not living a life in the spirit, Paul speaks of the 'fruit[s] of the spirit', which are the positive signs of the spiritual life. Note that 'joy', **charâ**, is classed with the virtues.

'Kindness', **chrêstotês**, differs from 'goodness', **agathôsynê**, in that the former is one aspect of goodness, i.e. being nice to people, while the latter is sheer goodness, where all one's actions are manifestations of moral integrity. **Chrêstotês** is often used in classical writers to describe soft-heartedness or kind naivety. **Agathôsynê**, a rare non-classical word, occurs in Eph. 5.9 along with 'righteousness', **dikaiosynê**, and 'truth', **alêtheia**. This indicates its generic nature and context.

[23] 'Gentleness', **prâÿtês**, Vulg. *modestia*, in classical

authors is often contrasted with irritability or bad temper, and denotes mildness and restraint.

'Self-control', **engkrateia**, Vulg. *continentia*, is control over one's desires or restraint in dealing with the temptations of pleasure. It later tended to denote particularly sexual continence. The second century sect of ascetics known as the Encratites abstained from meat, wine, sex and owning property.

'Against such there is no Law', i.e. the Law has no control over such things, it ceases to exist in the face of such things. As Lightfoot says, 'Law exists for the purpose of restraint, but in the works of the Spirit there is nothing to restrain.'

[24] The verb 'to be' is omitted, as is general in Greek with such phrases involving the use of a definite article followed by a prepositional phrase. We could also translate **hoi tou Christou** as 'the [people] of Christ'. Some early commentators strangely took 'the flesh' with 'of Christ', i.e. 'have crucified the flesh of Christ'. It is difficult to see what such an interpretation could mean. The Vulgate, however, correctly reads *qui autem sunt Christi, carnem crucifixerunt*. This concept of the believer sharing in a mystical sense in the crucifixion of Christ is picked up again by Paul in 6.14, 'the cross of our Lord Jesus Christ through whom the world has been crucified to me, and I to the world'. As we have died and been raised with Christ in baptism, our 'flesh' or old self can be said to have been crucified along with Christ.

'Troubles', **pathêmasin**, are the general things the flesh suffers from or is affected by. 'Desires', **epithûmiais**, are particular things by which the flesh is affected.

[25] Since the spirit has given us life, we are obliged to make our way of life one that is harmonious with the spirit. Note that Paul again uses the plain instrumental dative here (**pneumati**),

and not **en** with the dative, which would mean much the same, i.e. 'in' or 'by'.

[26] 'Conceited', **kenodoxoi**, literally, 'vain-glorious', describes individuals who not only think a lot of themselves but who also behave in a selfish way.

'Provoking', **prokaloumenoi**, is from a verb used in a military context meaning 'challenge to a fight'. The connection between aggressive behaviour and 'vain-glorying', **kenodoxiâ**, might strike us as an odd association of ideas, but Phil. 2.2–4 provides a similar context for **kenodoxiâ**, 'Complete my joy by having the same mind and the same love, by sharing the same soul, having one mind, [doing] nothing motivated *by intrigue* (**kat'erîtheiân**) or *conceit* (**kata kenodoxiân**), but humbly treating the other person as superior to oneself, with each one of you looking out not for his own but other people's interests as well.'

'Bearing grudges', **pthonountes**, fits the context better than 'envying', the usual translation of this word. 'Harbouring resentment' is an alternative translation.

Chapter 6

1 Brothers and sisters, if any person is also caught out in some failing, you who are divinely inspired should set such a one right again in a spirit of gentleness, watching out for yourself lest you too be tempted. 2 Bear one another's burdens and in this way fulfil the Law of Christ. 3 For if anyone thinks he is something when he is nothing he deceives himself.

[1] 'Caught out', **prolêmpthêi**, i.e. 'detected', rather than the more literal 'caught beforehand', (AV) 'overtaken'.

'Who are divinely inspired', **hoi pneumatikoi**, are either those who are driven by the spirit, the spiritually minded, or those who have received the gift of counselling from the Holy Spirit. See I Cor. 2.15, 'The spiritual person (**ho pneumatikos**) can assess everything but is himself assessed by no one.'

'Set right again', **katartizete**, is often used in a medical sense of setting broken or dislocated limbs. It also means 'furnish', 'kit out', 'prepare'.

The singular 'yourself' has been retained in translation although it is ungrammatical. Paul starts with the plural form of 'you', **hûmeis**, together with the plural of the verb and slips into the singular for the last part of the sentence.

[2] 'Fulfil', **anaplêrôsate**, rather than 'you will fulfil', **anaplêrôsete**, which is found in some manuscripts.

'The Law of Christ' is contrasted with the 'Law of Moses', as we see elsewhere in Paul's works, e.g. Rom. 3.27, where he contrasts the Law of works with the Law of faith, and Rom. 8.2, where the Law of the spirit of life in Christ Jesus is set against the Law of sin and death. Similarly the unnecessary burdens of the Law are contrasted with those burdens which we should carry. The notion that the Mosaic Law was burdensome is seen in Luke 11.46, 'Woe to you upholders of the Law (**nomikois**), because you load people up with burdens that are hard to carry, and yet you yourselves do not touch these burdens with one of your fingers.'

[3] The underlying meaning of this verse is that someone who thinks too much of himself is unaware of the real meaning of the Law of Christ, which is that one should bear another's burdens. As I have said above, conceit is selfish behaviour, not just having an elevated notion of oneself.

4 Let each one think it right [to do] his own work, and then he will be able to be proud of himself alone and not someone else. 5 For each one will carry his own load. 6 Let the one being instructed in the word share all his goods with the one instructing him. 7 Do not be misled; God is not caught out. For a human being will reap whatever he sows. 8 Because he who sows in his flesh will reap destruction from the flesh, but he who sows in the spirit will reap eternal life from the spirit.

[4] 'Think it right', **dokimazetô**, a verb which usually means 'test', 'examine', but can also mean 'approve'. The meaning of this verse is that one should support oneself by work and not rely on others for support. Note that Paul sees nothing wrong in feeling proud of oneself when one has done something

praiseworthy. The Greek expression is quite strong: **kauchêma hexei**, 'will have something to boast about'.

[5] This verse reminds one of a proverb or saying, perhaps from a military context referring to soldiers carrying their own packs. It is a summary of the previous verse. The word for 'load', **phortion**, is often used metaphorically in classical writers as well as in the NT, e.g. Matt. 11.30, 'my load is light'.

[6] 'The one being instructed', **ho katêchoumenos**, from which we derive 'catechumen', is any church member who is receiving instruction from an appointed teacher of the church.

'The word' includes study of the scriptures, moral teaching and the preaching of the gospel.

'Share all his goods' (more precisely, 'give a share of all his goods', i.e. not 'give away all his goods'), **koinôneitô . . . en pâsin agathois,** refers to giving food or money to those who are spending their time on instructing the members of the church. The AV 'communicate unto him that teacheth in all good things' is confusing to a modern reader, who might think that it refers to sharing one's bright ideas. Although 'share' in the sense of 'tell other people what one thinks' is a modern idiom some people are fond of using, one should note that there is no case of such a usage in the NT.

[7] 'Caught out', **myktêrizetai**, rather than 'mocked'. The verb literally means 'to turn one's nose up at something', 'to look down on', but came to take on the sense of 'to cheat'. Despising leads to trying to get the better of someone. Our idiom 'to make a fool of' is close to the sense of this verb.

[8] The context in which the warning of God's judgment occurs is that of the duty of sharing one's possessions with others. Could Paul be alluding to the fates of Ananias and Sapphira (Acts 5.1–11)? 'Sowing in the flesh' in this context

clearly refers to cheating in the matter of sharing one's property, but what is the force of the metaphor? 'In his flesh', **eis tên sarka heautou**, is really '*into* his flesh'. In other words, the worldly person sows his seed into the soil of the flesh, investing in the material world, whereas the spiritual person sows his seed into the field of the spirit, from which he will harvest an everlasting crop.

9 Let us not neglect to do good, for in due time we shall reap if we do not become slack. 10 So then, as we get the chance, let us do good to everyone, especially to those in the family of faith. 11 See what large letters I have written to you with my own hand. 12 All those who wish to put on a good show in the flesh are forcing you to be circumcised, only in order that they might avoid persecution for the cross of Christ.

[9] 'Become slack', **eklûomenoi**, a verb used to describe such acts as unstringing a bow or letting oneself get out of condition.
   'In due time', **kairôi idiôi**, literally, 'in proper season'.

[10] 'Chance', **kairon**, this time in the sense of 'opportunity'. Is it possible to take the word in the same sense it has in the previous verse, i.e. as referring to the time when God will judge the world and reward the righteous? In other words, can we translate the opening part of this verse, **hôs kairon echomen**, 'as we have a time coming'? Alternatively, we can translate it as 'as we still have the time'. Ignatius (*To the Smyrnaeans* 9.1) gives support to the last interpretation with the clause 'while we still have time (for repentance)', **hôs eti kairon echomen**. It is difficult to decide, but I have followed Lightfoot, who sees the deliberate antithesis between **kairôi** in the previous verse and **kairon** here, but sees the two as referring respectively to a time for sowing and a time for reaping. Lightfoot translates 'as we

find a seasonable time, as opportunity presents'. This is the interpretation followed by the AV, 'as we have therefore opportunity'.

'The family of faith', **tous oikeious tês pisteôs**, literally, 'those in the household of the faith', i.e. fellow Christians. Already the word **pistis** is beginning to stand for the Christian faith, i.e. Christianity. The metaphor of the household is deliberately used to recall the OT references to Moses who was 'faithful in all my household' (Num. 12.7). The writer of the Letter to the Hebrews (3.2–6) develops this theme and says in v.6, 'But Christ is over his household as a son, whose household we are, if we continue steadfast, speaking freely and proclaiming our hope until the end' (see my notes on this passage in *Reading through Hebrews*).

The significance of the reference to the household is that the household of Moses is the nation of Israel. Paul has been trying to assure his audience that they are true sons of Abraham and have inherited the promises given to Abraham by God. Since he has concentrated in his argument up to now on the superiority of these promises compared with the benefits of the Mosaic Law, Paul has to assure by implication his audience of Gentile Christians that they still belong to the authentic household of Israel. The implication is spelled out in v.16.

[11] This verse and the succeeding verses were actually written personally by Paul. The previous part of the letter was written by a secretary. Paul seems to have been in the habit of adding a few words in his own handwriting, perhaps to assure the recipients of the genuineness of the letter, as most commentators suggest, but more likely as a personal gesture of love and concern. We all prefer to receive a private letter or a birthday card which has been personally signed by the sender.

Too much emphasis has been placed by some commentators on the risk of forgeries circulating in the early church. One passage, in particular, has often been put forward as evidence for the existence of forgeries, namely, II Thess. 2.2, ' . . .that you should not be quickly distracted from good sense or be disturbed, whether through a spiritual revelation, or a message or a letter *as* [something coming] *through us* (**hôs di' hêmôn**), that the day of the Lord is imminent'. The Greek has been translated as though it meant something like 'as though coming *from* us', i.e. 'purporting to come from us', but this is not correct. Paul is referring to the unfortunate effect of his earlier letter, which had been misinterpreted by its over-anxious recipients. Forgeries certainly appeared at a later date, such as the Letter to the Laodiceans and the Letter to the Alexandrians, but a cursory glance shows them to be very clumsy forgeries and the early church knew that they were. When we consider that the letters Paul or any other apostle wrote would have been conveyed to their recipients for the most part by trusted and faithful friends it is unrealistic to suppose that forgeries were prevalent. In the absence of any concrete evidence we should not let our imagination run riot.

'See what large letters I have written' probably refers not to the fact that the size of his handwriting was especially large compared with that of others but to the fact that his handwriting was that of an amateur and not that of a professional scribe who would have written neatly and economically, i.e. without wasting expensive paper. Some have seen in the reference to large handwriting evidence that Paul's eyesight was poor, and others have suggested that Paul is referring to his untidy or bad handwriting. The word he uses, however, is **pêlikois**, which can only mean 'how large'. Even the word 'letters', **grammasin**, has been misunderstood. The AV has 'how large a letter', as though Paul is referring to the length of his epistle, which is actually not particularly long. This interpretation must be rejected since the expression Paul uses is **grammasin egrapsa**, 'I have written *with* letters', not **grammata egrapsa**, 'I have written [a] letter[s]'.

[12] Paul imputes a new motive to the Judaizers; they are trying to avoid persecution as Christians by pretending to be Jews. This suggestion should not be dismissed out of hand. There can be no doubt that at the time Paul was writing Christians were regarded as trouble-makers compared with the Jews, who had been accepted in communities throughout the Roman empire for many years. Although there had been occasions when Jews were persecuted, as had happened in Alexandria where there were large numbers of Jews, in the main Jews were more acceptable than Christians. The Christian gospel with its talk of the kingdom of God and its egalitarian ethos was bound to be regarded as a threat to the *status quo*. Speculation about what Christians actually did at their 'love-feasts' would lead to accusations of immoral behaviour. The situation changed radically after the Jewish War broke out, after which Jews were no longer regarded as harmless foreigners.

'Put on a good show', **euprosôpêsai**, literally 'put on a good face'. This probably refers to the Judaizers currying favour with the authorities as well as with the Jews by representing the Christian church as just another form of Jewish synagogue. This would fit in with Paul's suggestion that they were trying to avoid persecution as Christians. This is a more likely interpretation than the usual one which takes the expression as referring solely to the Judaizers currying favour with the unconverted Jews or trying to impress God himself. Such an interpretation is ruled out by the reference to the real motive, 'that they might avoid persecution for the cross of Christ'.

13 For the circumcisers do not even keep the Law themselves, yet they want you to be circumcised, so that they can boast about your flesh. 14 Far be it from me to boast except of the cross of our Lord Jesus Christ, through whom the world has been crucified to

me, and I to the world. 15 For neither circumcision nor
non-circumcision is anything. On the contrary, there is
a new creation. 16 And on all those who will conform
to this rule, and on the Israel of God, [be] peace and
mercy. 17 Finally, let no one cause me suffering, for I
bear the marks of the Lord Jesus Christ on my body. 18
The grace of our Lord Jesus Christ [be] with your
spirit, brothers and sisters, amen.

[13] 'The circumcisers', **hoi peritemnomenoi,** i.e. 'those who
circumcise', a participle to be taken as middle, not passive,
which would mean 'those being circumcised' (in Greek the
middle and passive present participles are identical in form). If
it were a passive participle it would imply that they are Gentile
Christians who wish to be circumcised themselves. Since Paul
goes on to say that they 'do not even keep the Law themselves',
we must accept that they are Jewish Christians who are
hypocritical about their own observance of the Law. It would
be odd for Paul to criticize them for not keeping the Law if they
had never been circumcised. On the other hand, it is fairly clear
that Paul would see his opponents as a mixed group of Jewish
and Gentile Christians with Judaizing tendencies.

'Boast about your flesh', i.e. boast about their success in
winning people over to the observance of the 'fleshly' Law or,
more specifically perhaps, boast about the mutilation of your
flesh by having you circumcised.

[14] Boasting is not necessarily a bad thing, as we have already
seen in verse 4 above. Paul frequently speaks of boasting – he
uses the verb **kauchaomai** at least thirty-four times and the
noun **kauchêma** three times in II Corinthians alone, and mostly
in a good sense.

Celsus, the pagan writer who attacked Christianity in the
second century, is said by Origen (*Against Celsus*, 5.64) to have

commented on this verse, 'Men who differ so widely amongst themselves and attack each other so shamefully in their quarrels may all be heard using the expression "The world has been crucified to me and I to the world".' Origen's dry comment on this is worth quoting: 'This is the only sentence that Celsus seems to have remembered from Paul.'

[15] This verse has some surprising variations in the text. A large number of reputable manuscripts add at the start 'For in Christ Jesus . . .', probably a marginal note incorporated in the text. The addition is not found in a reliable early papyrus nor in other later but equally reliable texts. One or two texts also have **ischyei**, 'is worth', 'has force', instead of **estin**, 'is', but this variation is also to be rejected. The Vulgate is based on a text which includes both variations, i.e. *in Christo enim Iesu* and *valet*.

According to Lightfoot, 'new creation', **kainê ktisis**, is a translation of a common expression used by Jewish writers to denote someone brought to the knowledge of the true God. It is also found in II Cor. 5.17, 'So if one is in Christ, one is a new creation; the old things have passed away; look, they have been made new.' **Ktisis** in the NT can denote all that God created, i.e. the universe, as well as an individual creature as in this verse. Chrysostom certainly seems to interpret this reference as including the whole of creation: 'the heavens and the earth also together with *the whole of creation* (**pâsa hê ktisis**) will be changed into immortality along with our bodies.'

[16] 'Conform to', **stoichêsousin**, literally, 'will line up with'. This reading is preferable to **stoichousin** (present tense) found in some manuscripts because it stresses the need to continue to be faithful in the future.

'Israel of God', i.e. Christians, who are the true people of God rather than those who call themselves Israelites. This reference is meant to reassure the Galatians that they are true children of Abraham and heirs of the promise.

[17] 'Finally', **tou loipou,** which can also be translated 'henceforth'.

'The marks', **ta stigmata,** are the marks of ownership branded on the bodies of slaves. Paul is most probably referring to the scars which he carries from beatings, and, perhaps, the scars on his body which were caused by the stoning described in Acts 14.19. This stoning (see notes on 4.13) may have been the occasion for Paul's first preaching of the gospel to his audience. Paul is probably using the analogy of a slave dedicated to a god. Such slaves were regarded as sacred and in some cases not to be touched by anyone. It has also been suggested less plausibly that it refers to the practice of soldiers who sometimes branded (tattooed?) themselves with the name of their commander.

Chrysostom points out that Paul uses the verb **bastazô,** 'I bear', not **echô,** 'I have', because he is proud to display his scars as though they were trophies or royal standards.

[18] 'Brothers and sisters', **adelphoi,** unusually occurs in the emphatic position at the end of the sentence, before the final 'amen'. It has been suggested that this is an expression of tenderness to counteract the severe tone of the rest of the letter.

Bibliography

W. D. Davies, *Paul and Rabbinic Judaism: Some Rabbinic Elements in Pauline Theology*, SPCK ²1955

J. D. G. Dunn, *Jesus, Paul and the Law: Studies in Mark and Galatians*, SPCK 1990

R. H. Eisenman & M. Wise, *The Dead Sea Scrolls Uncovered*, Element Books 1992

C. W. Emmet, *St Paul's Epistle to the Galatians*, R. Scott 1912

D. Goldstein, *Jewish Legends*, Library of the World's Myths and Legends, Chancellor Press 1996

W. F. Knox, *A New Commentary on Holy Scripture*, SPCK 1958

J. B. Lightfoot, *Saint Paul's Epistle to the Galatians*, Macmillan 1900

J. Murphy-O'Connor, *Paul: A Critical Life*, Oxford University Press 1996

J. Sacks, *Faith in the Future*, Darton, Longman and Todd 1995

E. P. Sanders, *Paul and Palestinian Judaism: A Comparison of Patterns of Religion*, SCM Press 1977

J. N. Sanders, 'Galatians', *Peake's Commentary on the Bible*, Nelson 1962